THE BARON AND ROSA

Rosa Kende

ORIGINAL WRITING

978-1-907179-45-7

A CIP catalogue for this book is available from the National Library.

Published by Original Writing Ltd., Dublin, 2010.

Printed in Great Britain by the MPG Books Group, Bodmin and King's Lynn

14 August, 1956

ACKNOWLEDGEMENTS

Without Helen Erasmus and her huge commitment in the care of Gábor in his final years, I would never have been able to write these pages. Now she is sick herself and I know that Gábor would have joined with me now in expressing our gratitude for all she has done for us over the years.

I hope that one day my grandchildren Georges, Theo, Liberty and Tobias will accept and read this book, written specially for them in memory of their Grandpop and Grandma.

Daniel Morehead has also been a great help in the production of this book. Apart from being a top class graphic designer he is also our nephew, Daisy's first cousin and long time friend, son of my great friend Doreen Morehead his father is Gábor Kende junior, my husband's nephew. Daniel spent many days here in Newtown Donore during his youth, including nearly every Christmas, and has always been counted as a member of the family. Thank you, Daniel.

Newtown Donore,
Naas.

Contents

Introduction

Written by Daisy Jacquier-Kende, read by Conor Doyle at the Removal Service for Gábor Kende at Caragh Church Sunday 5th February 2006

My father was a stickler for accuracy and fine detail, often to the point of nail biting frustration. Many a story started with "Well, we woke at about 9, went downstairs and had boiled eggs for breakfast....". I well remember one recent Christmas he opened a present of a state of the art weighing scales from mama, he carefully read the label on the back which said "made in Singapore", he gave a gasp of admiration and exclaimed "and you know what, I bet it is deadly accurate". His sense of order was renowned by all who knew him, there were lists written daily and lists were called upon to tackle any situation.

Said weighing scales were used religiously every day at the same hour to check his state of health in the last years.

He was about as accurate himself throughout his life as anybody could be however he luckily was wrong about one idea of his. On the basis that each of his siblings had died below the age of 75 he found it absurd that anyone should expect him to live any longer than that age. Certain areas of life were affected by this prediction, namely the choosing of a car or a camera. Each car was bought on the fact that it would be needed for so many years prior to mama changing it for something more appropriate to a woman getting around on her own. Needless to say he survived several cars and cameras.

Weather and time were of huge importance to him. As a farmer it was vital to know what the skies would bring, and thankfully he made sure that anyone in the house would leave and arrive on time, woe behold if you didn't.

Papi loved proverbs, some of his favourites were "Never put off to tomorrow what you can do today", "Birds of a feather fly together", sometimes he would translate Hungarian or German ones for us if he could not find one in English to express what he wanted to say.

He loved people, people who were genuine, people who worked hard and who were guided by honesty and driven by a striving for excellence. He had a great and often bizarre sense of humour. There was one awful joke about a poor cat which was told at many a dinner party, the reason behind the punch line will always remain a mystery.

So many of you have called or arrived at the house over the course of the past couple of days showing huge remorse but above all an enormous fondness for a man who has unwittingly shared with you his unique courage and wisdom. Thank you for coming and calling and sharing your memories of him with us.

As I noted down some words and adjectives over the past few days which I thought were fitting to describe him I found some stark contradictions. He was modest and discreet, he wore his heart on his sleeve; he was polite and charming, he was incredibly rude; he was a man of few words, he voiced his strong opinions readily; he was rational to the last, he could be totally bloodyminded; he was a man of moderation and measure, he indulged to excess; he was meticulously tidy, his desk was always a mess; he had huge courage and bravery, he could at times be a most difficult patient; he loathed what he called "new fangled objects", he welcomed change, for years never missing an episode of "Tomorrows World"; A man from the past, a man of the future.

What he was was true to himself. He knew and followed his own mind throughout his long full life. He never doubted himself, he never had to.

He never forgot anyone whom he had met and he loved hearing news of old friends. Opening the Christmas cards each year gave him huge pleasure, he would read each one aloud, slowly, sitting at the kitchen table.

He deeply loved and cherished the family and extended family.

Above all it is his courage, wisdom and charm which will live on, which will keep him alive for all of us here.

I am so lucky to have had you as my father Papi, thank you and goodbye. I am proud of you. I love you.

BOOK 1
THE DOYLE FAMILY

Elsa

I

EARLY DAYS IN MENLOE AND DRUMCORA

We stayed with our grandparents for six months in Drumcora at a time when our own house was being reconstructed. Drumcora and Menloe were on opposite sides of the Blackrock Road in Cork. Our father Tom Doyle had married our mother Ita O'Donovan in 1931, and there were four of us, all girls, all under five, one for each season of the year. I, Rosemary, was Autumn, Ita was born in Winter, Ann in the Spring, and lovely summer welcomed Ruth into the world. We were born in a house opposite the University. My parents sold the house on acquiring the ruins of Menloe House, a house burnt down sometime in 1936. Hence we stayed with our grandparents whilst our own place was being renovated.

I can still see the white stones lining the avenue to Drumcora, with iron fences marking fields that led to the river below, fields where Simon Mick grazed. He was our father's hunter. His stable was near the house, easy for little people to visit and try to help Paddy, the groom. Another favourite place was the conservatory. It was very Victorian and large, housing what seemed to be *thousands* of heavily smelling plants (to a very young member of the family). The grownups used to sit there and have tea. One could quite easily be unnoticed behind a plant. Basketwork chairs were dotted around.

Another memory of Drumcora was that of sitting under the dining-room table whilst the old people dined. The children ate in the nursery – they have no memories of eating in the dining room, but I do remember being under the dining-room table, stroking the fungus that grew softly on long forgotten pieces of food! It was a fungus that grew like the stamen of a flower. Ruth had the same fascination for things unhygienic. There was a religious intensity about our absorption. Two children stroked their little plants, never hurting them nor breaking them. The plant's soft caress against tiny hands was enough reward for looking after them. As a matter of fact, it never occurred to us that they were "dirty" – this was a completely undiscovered concept!

In the hall there was a tiger skin with a stuffed head, an empty body and a long tail. This was another joy. Taking turns to sit on its head, we would drag the poor animal by its tail all around the polished floor. There were lots of pieces of furniture in that room, all dark and exciting. The sitting room was different – it had modern furniture and opened onto the conservatory. It was in the sitting room that our grandfather lined up the four children to receive sweets on Saturdays. We did not get many – and that was our limit for the week. I was about four at the time, with Ann as the oldest and the others, Ita and Ruth, younger. Imagining how it was, it was very good of our grandparents to have had us there. Our Aunt Kay was in charge of the house and did a marathon job with the help of a very kind girl called Mina. The dining table always had a green baize cloth on it, and two of the children were glad that the floor underneath was never investigated!

There is a photograph taken, one would imagine, at a wedding – everyone dressed up in morning clothes; vague faces looking at the camera. Some faces are easy to recognize, Aunt Maureen and Aunt Bessie for instance. It is more difficult to know our mother – she did not take a good photograph. However, there is a photograph of her at her wedding, looking elegant in a beautiful dress.

....

Eventually the day came for the move to Menloe. The move to Menloe was a move into a furnished house. It was bright and welcoming. Drumcora was rather dark. Houses built on that side of the river faced north whereas Menloe had the gaiety of a southern aspect. Our first Victorian house had also been pretty dark so, without analyzing it, we children ran and ran screaming loudly, joyful and excited. Sleeping that first night in new beds was both warm and comforting

Our mother, Ita, loved to play hockey. She was on the Munster team. Strangely enough, when we were older Ann and I also played without knowing that our mother had been so good at the game. Whilst at school we both represented the South East. I am not sure whether we were all that brilliant but I suspect we had little opposition. It is still strange that we managed to achieve something that our mother would have enjoyed, without our having the slightest idea of her success in the same field.

Our father, Tom Doyle hunted with the Sean Peels on Sundays. There were some who found the idea of Sunday hunting repellent. Most of the land owners at that time were Protestant and they set the rules for Sundays! Protestant women were not even allowed to sew on that holy day. They would have starved if they had not had Catholics in the kitchen. The Sean Peel hunt was looked upon with horror, but Tom Doyle and Sean Hyde enjoyed themselves hugely with their Catholic friends.

Tom's other love was sailing. With his friend Harry Donegan's father, a great yachtsman known universally as Skipper Donegan, Dad sailed on *The Gull* until he bought *Sybil*, a Cork One Design boat. The One Designs were fifty years old, and at the time were still racing every week. Not only fine racing vessels, they were also a family boat with plenty of space. Dad changed to a bigger boat as the necessity for more civilised outings became apparent. *Elsa* sported five bunks and a galley. An engine made the catching of moorings less of a hazard!

Cork Harbour has the reputation of being only second to Sydney in beauty. The lovely town of Cobh flanked the entrance to the river Lee, as it entered the sea. Its tall cathedral graced the bay that sported its islands of Spike and Haulbowline. The Royal Cork Yacht Club was in Cobh, but unfortunately it could no longer provide the necessary haven for yachts, with the ever increasing traffic of merchant ships. The Club moved to Crosshaven in the 1960s, and the Royal Munster Yacht Club became the Royal Cork Yacht Club, the oldest yacht club in the world.

Tom worked in the city. He and his father Denis had a stevedoring business, so he had to leave home very early in the morning. Our mother was as thrilled about the house as the children. Little Rosa liked to follow her Mum upstairs, walking up the stairs behind her, imitating her as she prepared to go to the loo – as they walked they lifted their skirts. I remember sitting with her and Ann upstairs in a bus, going home to our house on the Western Road. We spotted our Dad's car down on the road, and our mother started to panic, realizing that we were late coming home. I hope that the bus won that little race!

Recently, I needed a birth certificate and was unable to understand why the Public Record Office could not find me in the records. They phoned finally to tell me that they had recently computerized the system, and no home births had been included as yet. I was thrilled to hear that I had been delivered at home. (Calls for buckets of hot water and plenty of warm towels surrounded that little me as I pampered my way into this world!) I hoped that I had not made my mother suffer too much. I remember going for walks with our Nanny around nearby housing estates. Another memory that I have is that a wasp got stuck in my ear. Everyone was terrified, and a taxi was called to take me to the nearest hospital. I remember sitting with my mother as she cautioned, "Don't move, don't move." In the hospital everything seemed white and quiet. I felt nothing until they said it was all over. Another joust with the hospital system was when my tonsils were removed. It happened in a nursing home that was, in fact, an ordinary house. I was in one bed in that big room, and my mother, on the other side of the room, in a second. I insisted on having my tonsils placed in a jar and put on the mantelpiece.

Denis Francis Doyle
(Grandfather)

Mary O'Donovan,
with her daughter Ita

Daniel O'Donovan,
(Grandfather)

Wedding of Tom Doyle and Ita O'Donovan 4th April, 1931
Bridesmaids, Cathy O'Donovan, Maureen Doyle
Bestman, Harry Donegan
Parents of Tom Doyle and father of Ita, plus 4 priests

Ita Doyle

Ita Doyle with Rosa and Ann

Menloe House

Garden in Menloe

Garden in Menloe

2

Our grandfather died in 1938. Although no politician, he supported the Fine Gael party. At that time, and later, the Fine Gael party roughly represented those who had been for the Treaty of 1921. He was very much against the IRA and DeValera. He actually sent his son, Tom, to Belgium for the duration of the Civil War so that he might divert him from any temptation to join the dare-devilry of his friends. Denis Doyle lived on the Victoria road at that time. It was his joy to allow Michael Collins to use his house for secret meetings. This information came from Kay Buckley, our aunt.

There is a story told of Grandad that he raced hay from all around the country to reach the boats going to France with fodder for the horses of the British cavalry. Evidently his friend O'Sullivan had the same idea, and thus whoever got to the boats first was able to send his hay abroad. It is probably true, since Grandad had a stevedoring company in Cork. He was also a very benevolent man with huge interest in the welfare of others. His mother, a Coakley, was matron of the hospital in Middleton. The Coakleys were excise men in the port of Cork in the nineteenth century. Because his mother was away so much, Denis Doyle was reared by his mother's sister, Aunt Liz. It was her daughter, Lil, who was known by all the grandchildren. He had a sister, Matilda, about whom I know nothing.

Speaking of houses, the three houses that were Denis Francis Doyle's own property during his lifetime reflected his success as a businessman. The older children, including our father Tom, were born in a tiny, one-storied house in Turner's Cross. That area has since become a motley of roads. The house only just escaped the developers, so it is possible to see that Denis and Annie Doyle had a difficult time as newly married and young parents. Hard work and enterprise intervened. Denis Noel, my father's brother arrived later. He was born in Drumcora and grew up to become a world-famous yachtsman.

Granny Doyle told a story about her husband's first success in business. Arriving home one day, he moaned about his inability to buy some wood that was piled up on the quays. He just did not have the money. His wife asked how much he would need and surprised him by producing a cache that she had been accumulating for just such an event. She had put aside for several years a small amount from her housekeeping money. It was enough and she took the credit for all that came later. The four grandchildren remember their grandfather as kind and loving. He was a giving person. His father, William Doyle, became famous when, in a drunken state, he blew up the gas works! Another story was that he took a pot shot at the King Edward V11 when he came to Cork and then escaped punishment by running away to America dressed as a woman. We would like to think that he did both those things! It is no wonder that his wife had to work in her hospital, all her life, and lucky that his child inherited her work ethic.

During those years of the 1930s the family had three summer houses in Poulgorm. The main house belonged to Denis and Annie, another house to Tom's family, and a third to the Scotts. The Hegartys, Aunt Pat and Uncle Frank, had a house within walking distance, in Fountainstown. The Donegans, Uncle Harry and Aunt Bessie, visited with frequency. Poulgorm is by the sea, opposite Ringabella, at the mouth of Cork Harbour. It has a very rocky inlet, with a beach of pebbles. What joy it was to go there and here it was that Granny was the star. She loved periwinkles and she loved telling stories. The stories were told not only once. Like a mantra they were repeated. I remember some.

She loved her husband and she loved to tell about their meeting. She was working in the family shop in Limerick when one day there was a tinkle as someone opened the door, and she saw him. As he walked towards her their eyes met. She suddenly knew what love was as she lost her tongue and could not remember the price of anything. He spoke and she was lost. She gave him what he needed and he turned to go out. Ah! Before he left he turned and said goodbye. He came back every week until they were married on 18th January, 1902, in the church of St. Michael, Limerick city.

One day, again in her shop, she heard a huge commotion in the street. Rushing outside she felt a terror, the like of which she had never experienced before. Huge men, brandishing sticks were running towards her. Like lightning she dashed back, pulled blinds, and hid, praying that they would go away. They did, but she never forgot the horror she felt that day. We listened as she told her stories and remember them into our own old age. These men were part of an Irish - style pogrom in Limerick at the turn of the century. The name Bérnard sounded Jewish. I traced the family, with the help of a genealogist, back to the end of the eighteenth century, but was unable to find any Jewish connection. Denis, our uncle, said that the family had changed its name in the 1790s. His habit of teasing made me doubt his veracity. At that time there was a family of Jewish descent named Bernal in Limerick. Harry McDowell, genealogist, could find no connection between the two families.

What Harry did find, however, is interesting. Music and photography were among the occupations in which the family was interested. I remember my Grand Uncle Paul. He and his brother helped in the reconstruction of Menloe. Paul played the violin and was wont to practice his instrument on the roof of their house in Limerick! It is said that he was one of the importers of the nine Stradavarii that came to Ireland at the turn of the nineteenth and twentieth centuries. Many people told me that he had it but what became of it I have no idea.

11

The inlet of Poulgorm was surrounded by black rocks on both sides. It made a charming swimming pool, the rocks' reflection turning the sea black. The men of the family built paths and viewing stands on the rocks, and there we would sit watching competitions between members of the family as they dived into the inky water with the greatest panache. At the age of two, in my excitement, I fell down the steps of the stand to the bottom and broke my collar bone. This brought about great consternation, but fortunately the oldest boy, Billy, was a doctor, and well able to stitch and repair. I was accident prone, and nobody was in the least surprised when a cut on my finger became septic. The cure in those days was to bathe it every day in boiling water. My response was to faint, each and every time that they tried to help me. Eventually they waited for me to faint and then did the bathing.

The last summer that we all spent together was in 1940. The sea was calm and the sun shone and poor Granny was sad. She wore black and yet took the hazardous path down to the little beach with her grandchildren. As she sat on the pebbly sand, she rocked with the sound of the sea. As it retreated, it picked up little stones with a sigh- whoosh! Coming in it made a similar sound but not quite the same. Granny seemed to rock in rhythm to the sea. Her husband had died four years previously and she was still bereft Back at the house all was different. The periwinkles they had collected and taken to Granny's house were boiled. Each of the children had a safety pin, and the shells were put on a plate on the floor. We speared the little fish and ate them. Bread and butter completed the feast.

After lunch one Sunday, we left the table and, gazing at the sea, young Denis called out that he had spotted a periscope! It was September 1939, and everyone spoke of war. Germany was the enemy and it seemed logical that the Germans should invade Ireland as a stepping-stone to England. Gazing where he pointed I saw it too. It became part of my memories for life. Years later, Denis confessed to having lied and robbed poor me of a cherished and scary moment!

1938 saw the start of primary school for Ann and me. We did not have far to go. There was a convent school just about two miles away. Dad still had his car and would take us and fetch us. When we got home we would play in the garden if the weather was kind. One day we were warned that our mother would not be at home when we arrived. She was about to have a very minor operation.

It was a lovely day that day in November. Ita and Ruth were playing in the garden with me. Three figures appeared at the side of the house – Ann, crying inconsolably, with Aunt Kay and Dad holding her. That tableaux has remained with me. Someone said that our mother was dead. My mind felt joyful as I understood that my beloved mother was with God. I could not understand why Ann was crying. The teaching of the nuns had indoctrinated me to such an extent that I felt that it would be wrong to begrudge my mother to God. It was her luck to be taken. The two smaller children were also happy as I explained. I had no concept of loss and no knowledge of bereavement. That would come later. I did not want to disturb our mother's happiness. That was a good Catholic way of treating such a monstrous tragedy Mother had died from an overdose of anaesthetic. Our poor father wanted to kill the anaesthetist who had taken our mother's life, but was restrained from doing so by his brother-in-law, Dan O'Donovan. Dan spent a few nights with Dad until he had calmed down.

A month later Ita, my sister, got diphtheria and was in bed right through Christmas. I slept in the same room. One night Ita was asleep, and our dear, dead mother crept silently into the room. She had been accustomed to say good night in this manner. She bent over Ita and made a sign of the cross on her forehead. She stood for a few moments whilst I waited for her to turn to me. She didn't: she left and I felt a surge of jealousy that I had never felt before. I was five years old and Ita was just four. Our mother Ita was only thirty-four when she died, and Ita, our sister, was killed in a car crash when she was only thirty-four.

Christmas party 1939

Ruth, Rosa, Ita, Ann with their father

3

It is impossible to remember the first impressions of my father because he has always been there.   My mother's death left him in sole charge of four little girls, ranging from six down to two. At the age of five to see a man, especially your father, cry is devastating. All I could do at that moment was to offer him a sweet and a kiss as he started his new role of father and mother.

We had a nanny, and two of us went to school. The nanny had a raucous voice and a cruel streak.   I spent many miserable hours hiding from her in a tree in Shady Lane. Shady Lane was a lane leading from the avenue through a small wood. I cannot remember if the nanny ever looked for me, but there I would stay until I heard the car coming home. The key in the lock at six o'clock signaled a scurrying of little feet from every corner of the house – one to take his hat, one his coat, and another to fetch his slippers.   Ruth, the youngest, carried his shoes away "to have a smile put on them".

Saturdays were special. Anything could happen. During the winter Dad usually drove us around Cork city and its environs. He had a deep love for the city and county, combined with quite an extraordinary knowledge of their history. Another favourite trip was to see the tiny house where he was born in Turner's Cross.   Sometimes we went to the sea, to enjoy its majestic anger or its still greyness, deserted by the wise during winter storms.

We had three stables in Menloe, always a firm requisite for Dad. Mossy, our groom, lived in the gate lodge with his father Paddy, who was the gardener. Years later I saw Mossy dressed as a Franciscan friar, begging for the order in Cork City.   I never heard his story, but would be very glad to know how it was he turned from horses to religion. We always had a pony that pulled the trap during the war and fulfilled our riding needs. Naturally the trap was used by everyone including our father, who organised stables in Crosshaven so that his sailing would not be interrupted. To go hunting meant hacking, usually involving miles of road, to get to the meet. Bicycles were the other mode of transport

Amongst the horses, Simon Mick was always the favourite; Radiance followed later. There was also a grey who had been the Champion at the Royal Dublin Society (RDS), but he had bad feet and ultimately had to be put down. Simon Mick lasted for a very long time and was eventually retired on our land. It was my father's wish that when Simon Mick died he should be buried on the land. However, in the end an easier method of disposal took over. Dad also hunted with the South Union on Tuesdays and Fridays. We waited for him at home and leapt into action at the sound of his horn coming up the avenue. He would stop and there he would stay. A steaming hot bath was prepared by one of us; another of us would certainly prepare a bran mash for Simon Mick; Mossy would walk the horse. The remaining two would ease a groaning father from his muddied car. He nearly always fell out hunting, sometimes quite seriously, but he kept going, and hunted well into his sixties.

....

During the holidays, we sailed with our father, and the summer house changed to Currabinny. I had my own little boat. Ann and I had come to an agreement without any legality. She "owned" the horses and I "owned" the boats. In our cognisance she had three horses and the odd mare, and I had *Curlew*, *Elsa*, the punt and the motorboat. Actually I did not care very much for the motorboat, but the punt was an essential. All necessities had to be brought by punt from Crosshaven. We also used it for fishing when the mackerel arrived. Fishing was not my favourite sport, but I had to go along to kill the fish, a task no one else cared to do. In those days the sea was clean and fresh, and mackerel were delicious.

For me sailing was my love and my life. I knew every boat in the harbour of Crosshaven and all the hands on the bigger yachts. Dad introduced us to the sport. He took us out on his boats, *Sybil* first, then *Elsa*, followed by *Sonata*, and finally in the last two years, *Sonatina*. He sailed on Wednesdays, Saturdays, and Sundays. Only Sunday was a full day. People worked a half day on Saturdays. During the rest of the week I had the use of my Uncle Denis's 12' International Dinghy – *Curlew*. Doreen Morehead sailed with me. She actually sailed the boat when we were racing. Nobody took us seriously at first, and we were given the unprecedented handicap of fifteen minutes in our favour. Naturally we won everything! As we crossed the line, the other sailors were holding up the bar in the club but spared a moment to raise a guffaw for the two lassies! Doreen remained a good friend until her death three years ago. The very reason why I had to crew in our partnership was the reason for her untimely death – a weak heart.

Possibilities to be pondered on a day's outing included such enchantments as East Ferry, Cobh, Monkstown, Ringabella, White Bay, or, perhaps, if the day were propitious, even further afield to the Daunt Light Ship, Ballycotton, or even Kinsale on the odd occasion. The greatest joy of these endlessly calm days of one's youth was listening to our Dad's ritualistically retold stories prompted by the ever-changing landscape. All were true, some from Napoleonic times, others from the time of the Troubles.

A ship called the Celtic foundered on the rocks on her way home from America. Dad was aboard, but not yet married. He heard the screaming passengers and on deck the band aiding them on their next journey with a magnificent rendering of "Nearer my God to Thee". He had carefully packed his suitcase before going on deck, but, to his horror, he found that he had forgotten his watch. He tried to return to his cabin but was prevented. Back on deck he saw, to his astonishment, that the ship was firmly resting on Roches Point, a light house opposite Poulgorm! To the accompaniment of "Nearer My God To

Thee", he nonchalantly stepped ashore and made his way home. Many years later he came across a group of divers searching the wreck of the Celtic. To the astonishment of one of the divers Dad yelled across the water, "Did you by any chance come across a gold watch down there?!"

Racing was taken very seriously. There was a deathly hush on board as skipper and crew worked out tactics, based on weather and tide. Putting up the spinnaker was tense, as was the approach to a buoy. None but the skipper took the tiller for racing. To give an idea of the tension built up as they reached the starting line, I recall another little story. Boats of diverse size and description tacked in every direction during a regatta, waiting for the moment of truth to arrive, the starting gun. As *Elsa* thundered past, they either ignored, or did not notice, a capsized dinghy in the water. Later that evening the joke of the Club was that the little boat was none other than *Curlew*, the property of Tom Doyle's daughter Rosa (me), with her friend Doreen Morehead!

Jokes became standard rituals. Another that Dad liked to remember was the day that I put *Sonata* aground. My immediate reaction was to shout, "My God, we're aground, and there's no whisky on board!" It became a great favourite of his.

The Royal Munster Yacht Club in Crosshaven was a great gathering place for tired and thirsty sailors. We had a house in Currabinny – on the opposite side of the river. Our job was to fetch our father home, when he phoned. I remember evenings of haunting calm on the river, accentuated by the strident blare of the Merries playing music, perhaps the song of the moment "Now is the Hour". Somehow the crazy accustomed noise even exaggerated the silent 'whoosh-whoosh' of our oars. Reaching our destination there was a pause, until, at last, guided by a good friend ("careful now Tom"), Dad was levered into the stern of the boat. We rowed him home as he sat, secure in the role of coxswain, warm after an evening of brandy and soda.

. . . .

I have not spoken as yet of my father's deep wisdom, his enormous charity and love; neither have I spoken of the four major tragedies in his life and how he bore them.   He was a man of integrity, whose aim was to instill in all of us children values that were idealistic and generous.   One of his precepts was to "be yourself, be natural".   I think that he was successful in his teaching.   It was very seldom that anyone in difficulty left him without help, when they came in need.   He never forgot his beginnings in Turner's Cross nor what he owed to his city and his country.   Investments to a man of the 1920s had to be in Ireland and could never be sent to another country, when the surplus had been made here. Dad had a love of learning that was with him to the end of his days, yet he never boasted of his great knowledge of history for instance.   He would listen to those interested in the acts of Irishmen in the past, or the Boer war, or Gallipoli in the First World War, whatever.   He would listen and learn, without pontification.   He was always interested in others' opinions.

I was with him after my sister died in a car crash.   All his preoccupation was for me – Ita and I had been very close.   We sat together behind her coffin, and I could not stop whining.   I knew his grief was enormous, but he took the role of father and kept trying to help me.   Before we took her to Dublin, we had an afternoon at home in Donore.   Neighbours were kind; it was just before Christmas, and cakes, drinks and a turkey arrived. I remember how wonderful Joy Weld was in helping us to overcome our reluctance to eat. I remember Lydia Watchorn arriving with that turkey. I remember Charlotte Bielenberg being so affectionate and interested.   Joy, Lydia and Charlotte were all neighbours and friends.

Dad had had practice at tragedy.   He was quite young, in his mid-thirties, when his father died. To lose a father is always difficult, but to be left in charge of a large family and their offspring

19

was hard. Dad loved them all and looked after them when they needed him. His grief at losing his father was something I never discussed with him, but, by implication, I knew it was one he had to live with. Our mother's death followed shortly, just two months later. That embraced the added sorrow of suddenness. She was in perfect health the day before. It was no wonder that a man who had lost his young wife the year before should try to help a sister-in-law who was saddened by separation from her husband. At the beginning of the war, Dad's brother, Billy, who was a doctor of medicine, was involved with the army and had to leave home. His wife was sent to live in Drumcora with her children. Dad felt sorry for her and tried to cheer her up. She should have realized that he was trying to alleviate his own loss also, by helping her. Later she took upon herself to describe his actions as being reminiscent of Pollyanna. It is sad how little people understand one another. Dad's third tragedy was in the loss of his best friend and brother-in-law, Harry Donegan. Harry was drowned off the shore of Dunlaoghaire. His body was found three weeks later in Wales. It was Dad who took on himself the dreadful task of looking for the body. His hearing was badly affected, and it took some time to recover his balance, because of damage to his middle ear, through stress.

....

Years passed, marriage and living in Peru kept me away. Then we bought a farm in County Kildare, and, until his final illness, my father never failed to come and see us once a month or more.

4

A wonderful day came when Dad brought home a beautiful new mother for us in 1941. Elsie Walsh, or Mum, as we came to call her, was from Charleville, and had three sisters. Two of the sisters, Charlotte and Augusta, married Fez Byrne and Sean Hyde respectively. Dear Hilda, who came to live with us, never married. Later she moved to the Hydes as Augusta's family got bigger.

Sean's brother, Paddy Hyde, died when riding in a Point-to-Point. His four girls became part of Sean's family. Because of the big connections on both sides, we saw a lot of each other both at home and in Flower Lodge. We rode together and played together. In those days we could walk the fields between the two houses. This came to an end when the Hyde girls went to live with their sister Mary.

....

Elsie Walsh was our riding teacher in the beginning, until she became our new mother. We went for lessons every week, and she taught us all the little tricks "heels down, straight back, and look through your pony's ears". Ann was the best rider from the start, heralding her great commitment to the horse during her lifetime. I liked it but lacked Ann's talent. She was by far the sportier of us two: better at swimming, better at hockey and now the better rider. Our pact in future years, that the horses were hers and the boats mine, was based on talent.

We were thrilled when Dad invited Elsie to be our stepmother. We longed for the day that she would join us, and at long last it came. All the uncles and aunts came to our house to celebrate their arrival back from their honeymoon in Parknasilla, a lovely hotel in west Cork. The party proved to be somewhat of an anticlimax when our new Mother disappeared upstairs with a headache. Dad coasted between Mum and the guests, embarrassed and contrite as he saw all that had been prepared. The guests left and we went to bed.

To this day I am ashamed of what happened when I was walking down Patrick Street on my way home from school. I saw my grandfather O'Donovan behind me, and he saw me. He was walking with the aid of a stick but unsteadily, and he started to wave it whilst calling me "Rosemary"! My shame is that I ran, somehow translating his love into my fear. Why did I do such a heinous thing? You see, I never saw him again. There were conflicts within the new marriage, conflicts that were based on the difficulties facing our step mother vis-à-vis our mother's relations. Like many children would be, I was bewildered by this They had behaved badly towards Mum, and we were doing all that we could to try and make her happy Yet I wish that I could turn back the clock and greet him with affection.

I was fascinated by Elsie's violin playing, and longed to learn. In response she bought a half size violin for me, and I started to play with Mr. Brady. I also learnt the piano. At that time the violin was my preferred instrument, and Mr. Brady entered me in the Feis Ceoil, the annual music competition in Ireland. It was a disaster! No sooner did I see the stage than I felt very sick. Mum rushed me to the street where I threw up everything in my stomach. My performance afterwards left a great deal to be desired! I accepted the fact that I was unable to perform in public and endeavoured to keep my instruments as my own escape route, a function that they continued to perform for much of my life. There was a time when, without instruments, music left me. Without it I was bereft, and, after some time did what I could to regain it. It is a forgiving talent, and, at least, my deep appreciation has returned.

One of my strongest memories is of Mum and Dad putting their bicycles on the train to Dublin with the intention of cycling out to Leopardstown for the races, in the suburbs of Dublin, a long way from Cork. There were so few cars on the road at the time that it made the expedition less daunting than it would be today.

All was not well in the relationship between Elsie and us girls. It must have been extremely difficult for her to marry into a family with four children under the age of ten. Small irritants took on large proportions, and, added to these, little Ruth who had lost her mother at the age of two, lost the ability to speak. A tutor was engaged, and, little by little, Ruth recovered. Poor Elsie had her own problems and could not comprehend what was happening.

A new Nanny came to look after us. Her name was Pauline and she was quite wonderful. Kind and loving, she looked after us in a way we had not known during the first years after our mother's early death. She became a real friend, not only to us but to Mum too. She was married to a chap in the. British Air Force and they both came from Passage West. He did not fly; he was a maintenance man on the ground. When he wrote she took his letter to her room to read. Her red eyes afterwards showed how much she missed him. Eventually she had to leave us to care for her sick mother. I took to racing buses, on my bicycle, from one point on the road to school to another, certain that if I won Pauline would not go. Doing that, I managed to break one of my front teeth, when I crashed into a lamppost. Anyway, Pauline did go, but I kept on racing buses in the hope that she would return. She did and she stayed with us until a year after the war ended. By then we had gone to boarding school, and my need was not so great. The babies had arrived and Pauline was occupied.

The babies, first Conor, and afterwards Elizabeth and Augusta, were not only the delight of us four but also of the entire school. The interest of the nuns and girls was quite astonishing. Everything about our babies had to be related after the holidays. Photographs had to be shown, and unashamed envy on the part of all our friends was to be seen to be believed! Each new sibling's birth was a major happening in the annals of the school!

In 1943 Ann and I went to boarding school in Waterford – the Ursuline Convent. Hearing now all the dreadful stories of abuse meted out to children in orphanages and other schools in the 1940s, our school was civilized and gentle in comparison, good at sport but scant in education. There was more interest in turning out "young ladies" than aspiring professionals! Our lives changed as we entered our teens. Towards the end of school, having done no work, I telephoned home and asked my father if he would mind if I did not pass the Leaving Certificate. Dad said "Not at all, you can always do it next year." This got me down to work in not uncertain fashion, three weeks before the exam.

I loved my school, the companionship, the sport, the music, and above all the laissez- faire attitude to scholarship. Reading novels was one of my favourite pastimes, and there was plenty of time to indulge it. There was very real joy in the friendships I made and in the rather innocent naughtiness that satisfied my need not to conform. Music was still my love, and I played the piano for hours every day. To achieve this I gave up all sciences, cooking and any other technical study that I could. I never remember being queried on this: there was a good acceptance of "talent" at the school, and the nuns could hear me practice in the music rooms when they were in church. My music teacher was Mother Agnes. She was Belgian, and her lovely room was decorated with photographs of the Belgian Royal family. Her father was conductor of the Court orchestra. She grew up in the Court. Her love of Queen Astrid, who had been killed in a car crash, was not only apparent in the display, but demonstrable whenever she spoke of her. Tears would appear before she turned back to our music. A person so full of love and music must have found Irish Jansenistic Catholicism and its consequent lack of any humanity difficult to bear.

Mother Agnes was steeped in music, and what I had to learn was hers by ingestion, from her own family. Her style was easy, that of an accompanist rather than a performer. She had such a deep knowledge that I found my impatience to play overcome as I listened to reasons why her father loved Beethoven. She never forgot the conductor as she spoke to me of the lives of the masters. King Leopold was still on her wall in 1945; it was not in her nature to blame him for what happened. His contrite and open grief allowed her to forgive him. Again and again I heard the story of how her beloved Queen died. They were going on a skiing trip on a dangerous road when she exclaimed as they rounded a corner at the beauty of the landscape. King Leopold lost concentration for a second, unfortunately long enough for the car to plunge over the precipice. His survival initiated years of remorse and grief. The world mourned Queen Astrid.

In addition to my exceptional piano teacher, I had a very special violin teacher as well. There were very few foreigners in Ireland at the time, least of all Germans. My teacher was a German speaker, but insisted that he was from Austria. His name was Hermann Gebler. He had studied in a Conservatoire in Germany and taught me in a similar fashion. He insisted on endless exercises, with no examinations and no scales. Music was only played at the end of lessons and was always sight read. If I had practised my exercises, he might have succeeded in making a violinist of me. As it was, even without exercise, I did not do too badly, but I enjoyed the school orchestra more than my lessons. Another contributing factor in what was a failure was the fact that the nuns insisted on my having a chaperone whilst being taught by a **MAN!!** The designated nun would sit there doing embroidery, pretending not to listen, all the while gathering material for the refectory that evening. It was a disaster!

Reading was a real joy also. The school had a very good library of the classics. Thackeray, Dostoevsky, Bronte, Scott were all devoured, and any others that I could find. A book was nearly always concealed within my study papers. Games were something I endured. I lacked the commitment necessary to be a winner! The idea of banging a ball hither and thither was rather boring, and "beating" someone in a game of tennis was not among my aspirations. As soon as I woke, my head filled with music, and all day sounds reverberated, picking up accompaniment from the endless series of chords that lived within me. Later that music would turn to literature and words. The amazing possibilities of definitions and stories all made for very little time for the real work-in-hand! A Maths teacher expressed her frustration with me when she said, "If Rosa Doyle would please descend from the sky; perhaps she could learn something with the rest of us."

When school ended all I wanted to do was to join an orchestra, or study music and English at university. Unfortunately my father's business was in the doldrums, and he felt that unless I went to Cork University, he might not be able to afford it. On top of that my sister Ann had given up her studies in Trinity after only one year. I was delighted at the idea of Cork, but Mum refused to have me stay at home. She had visions of us four sisters taking up residence for the foreseeable future! My disappointment was enormous, but I secretly made up my mind that if I was not going to be famous, I would be notorious. On that note I left for Dublin, and stayed for a year.

Dublin was great fun. I worked in a bank – an extremely dull occupation – until they asked me to leave after a stint in Tipperary. I met my second dear love, Chris Young, that year. Ours was a great passion, but he could not wait for my return from Tipperary. When I got back all was over, and it was time for me to move on to London. Clutching a suitcase and my fiddle, I had another friend, Eddie Comyns, drive me to the airport.

Before leaving Dublin I have to write something about our lives at that time – 1953/54. We lived on very little money, mine was usually topped up by Dad, who would give me enough for a dress or something else when he came to visit. Above all he would give me a meal. Food was the very last item on my mind – a packet of soup, suitably watered, would last for a week's sustenance. Boyfriends would supply the rest! They had cars, and it was customary in those days that a young lady had only to be decorative and a good companion to spend an evening with a young man. I think that I had plenty of boyfriends because I could make them laugh and feel good about themselves. To dance we went to hunt balls. These happened during the winter and were enormous fun. Waltzes, quick step and foxtrots, a few South American tunes such as the Pasa Doble, but, best loved of all, Irish dancing, were our joy as we twirled and hopped around the floor! My sailing was done from Dun Laoghaire and the Royal St.George Yacht Club, in a 14' dinghy.

Some acquaintance with the better restaurants in the city was mine, also thanks to my boyfriends. Cork had never been like this. There, if you went out with somebody, it was immediately assumed that marriage was in sight. Anonymity was a luxury to be found only in bigger cities. I enjoyed my time in Dublin and notched up quite a few points on my road to notoriety.

London brought the joy of walking barefoot in the street, of sailing on reservoirs, and on the Solent. Once again I had a boring job as assistant to an auditor. But life was good, and there were some great adventures. Of course I fell in love again – this time with Michael Stern who only confessed that he could never marry a Catholic when I was already head over heels. He was Jewish. He was a kind and lovely man, but I am sure that it was cowardice that stopped him from telling me about his inhibition.

Long nights were spent talking about politics, about philosophy and about our futures. The early 1950s were rather bleak in retrospect, but we were not alone in our dreams. Shaw, Beckett, Camus fed thoughts and ideas which were a long way from that school in Waterford. Endless chat about the effects of World War II and communism made us keen to speak to the young soldiers who had returned to study. There was a pub on the Thames to which we would go to meet young people on a Sunday. Drinks and chat would while away the afternoon.

A year and a half in London was nearly up, and it was time to meet my future husband. Such was the Rosa Doyle that met Gábor Kende in the Shelbourne Hotel in 1956 and sailed with him to Peru a few weeks later.

Wedding of Elsie Walsh and Tom Doyle
24th February 1941

Augusta   Elizabeth

- Conor and Parents

One designs racing, Kinsale

Doyle family at Conor's 21st Birthday party.

BOOK 2
THE KENDE FAMILY

Kölcsei Kende family

5

I sit and wait for the painters to finish what was begun four months ago. New windows are an amazing addition to the house, but the installation and finishing are a bore. Hopefully everything will be finished this week. During all this Gábor has been amazingly patient. He admits that he would never have done it himself. Now that he is so weak and sick he sleeps through it all, without comment and without rancour. That is not how I knew him.

Gábor Kölcsey Kende, my husband, was born in Cégénydanyad, in the County of Szatmár, Hungary, on 26th March, 1924, to Baron Gyorgy and Magdolna Kölcsey Kende. His childhood was ideal, loving and instructive. He had two brothers, Zsigi, and Gyorgy, and a sister, Éva. Zsigi and Éva were a few years older than Gábor and enjoyed having a little brother to spoil and to tease. Gyorgy had a playmate only a little younger than himself. To this day, Cégény is in a place both isolated and wild. The people one sees in the villages are descendants of soldiers, hold themselves as such, and have a presence and individuality evocative of galloping riders across the plains. The house looks out on parkland. The park, comprising some 100 acres of the 3,000 total, held many specimen trees including one plantain in front of the house that was so big that two people with outstretched arms could not, together, reach around it. There is a photo of six people trying to touch fingers, and failing! This famous tree is still there but, during the war the villagers denuded much of the park for badly needed fuel. They had no other way of keeping warm. They burnt their own furniture too, in that way ridding themselves of their servitude to the Baron and their own past.

The family crypt is in the park. Here generations of Kendes are interred. The last places were taken by the two Gyorgy. How apt it seems that, with the family evicted from their place, there was only room for the last two who had died in Hungary. Nowadays one approaches the house through the village, but in days gone by one drove through the park to the covered entrance of the house. This is an elegant pillared portal, large enough for a carriage and four.

A couple of tennis courts proved to be a great attraction for the neighbouring nobility, who, coming to tea, would play a little gentle tennis. For the more vigorous there was bathing in the river Szamos. The Szamos was kept at bay by a big dyke on one side of the house and village. In 1981 I had the opportunity of swimming there. The contained water was swift, an unusual experience for a sea baby like me! It was quite frightening at first as the water lifted one and pulled one onwards. To stop one had to literally dismount from the force of the river. It was an experience that had to be repeated again and again. Our daughter Daisy and I profited from it with gales of excited laughter. Unfortunately, when we returned in 1989 the water had allegedly been polluted by the Romanians – polluted by a factory upstream under their jurisdiction. This reflected the huge animosity between the Romanians and Hungarians. All of this is based on the disputed ownership of land. Transylvania was owned by Hungary until the Treaty of Yalta at the end of the war, when Churchill, Stalin, and Roosevelt divided Europe between the Russians and themselves. Western Europe eventually was returned to its rightful owners, but the countries in Eastern Europe had to suffer for another forty years before finally rising up and claiming back their sovereignty in 1989. The Romanians held on to Transyslvania, claiming a superior right through history. This is of course highly debateable and is still a controversial topic both in Hungary and amongst the many Hungarian inhabitants of the area.

The children's Grandfather, another Zsigmond, the original Baron, lived in Istvándi, about an hour from Cégény by carriage. Baron Zsigmond was a brilliant character who loved to flash around the county in a carriage with four white, perfectly matched, showy American horses, sporting long manes. He it was who organised, and executed, with his own money, the diversion of the river Szamos, thereby saving hundreds of acres from flooding in the spring. The flooding was caused by the river Tisza whose overflow created the Szamos. Zsigmond's project was to divert the two rivers into a straight line, dissecting the delta. It was a wonderful engineering feat. He was a great spender, rather profligate according to his son, but his efforts on behalf of his county earned him the title of Baron in 1916. It was said that, on his acceptance of the baronetcy, the family ceased to be the oldest of the nobility and became, instead, the youngest of the aristocracy.

Ilona, grandmother to the children, was a great favourite amongst them all. Always smiling, living in an enchanted setting, with a weir-made lake down a path from the garden, animals all around, the children could do no wrong. It was from her that Gábor inherited his big frame and eventual tendency to put on weight. Whenever he spoke of her, his eyes lit up in remembrance. She came from the Boer family who also came from Szatmár. Ilona's influence and laissez-faire attitude had a great deal to do with Zsigmond's popularity. He was a man of great sympathy and generosity, married to a woman loved by everyone. They had three children, Gyorgy, Katalin, and Gábriella. Kati Néni married into the Hódossy family, and Gábi became a Szemere. They remained close to the Kende family and often came with their children to Cégény. Both girls inherited land from the family, and, on top of that Gyorgy had to pay them a yearly sum as part of their dowry. In Hungary it was customary to endow the girls with an equal share of what was handed down to the boys. Realising that over the centuries the Kendes had been nearly wiped out as a family every few generations, it was wonderful that my father-in-law had three boys. He felt secure and dedicated his time to preserving as best he could his inheritance. His father's flamboyant lifestyle had left them impoverished, and he imposed a strict economic discipline on all members of the family.

Hero's Square in Budapest commemorates the four original Hungarians, invaders and settlers in 896. One of those is Ond – the original Kende. The name Kende itself is a title, meaning Leader. The second part of it, Kölcsey, may have been added much later. During the centuries the Kendes stayed in Szatmár County and developed the land. They fought to defend their property, but over the years, the acreage was depleted partly due to marriages, and maybe due to losses in battle. In the 1980s, near Cseke, a crypt was opened, and it was found to be an ancient burial ground of the Kende family. Because it was a considerable distance from Cégény the archaeologists were surprised. Gábor showed no such reaction. Within the family its history was known but they kept their past to themselves. All the documents of importance were lodged by us and by Éva in the Pannonhalma Monastery. It is here that the records of the oldest families are kept and preserved. An interesting fact is that a Kende signed the Hungarian Golden Bull in the 12th century. Students of genealogy or any interested will find details of this remarkable family in the monastery. Most of these records are in Latin. Latin was not only studied but also spoken by Hungarians in the past. My father-in-law was a fluent Latin speaker. When we met him in Austria in 1963 it was his pleasure to speak in this language, in our presence, to the local priest.

Gábor, Zsigi, Éva, Gyorgy

Baron Gyorgy Kende, with famous plantain tree

On Kende estate near
grandparent's house at
Istvandi

Cégény

Portal

Balcony looking on Park

Gyorgy in formal dress
for the Court

Baron Gyorgy junior,
killed at the siege of Budapest

Ilona Kende

Baroness Magdolna Kende

Wedding of Zsigmond Kende with
Madi Salomon

Their boys
Balint on the left and Gábor jnr right

43

Ferenc Kölcsei

6

Judith Listowel, a Hungarian novelist and historian found reference to a Kende, in the eleventh and twelfth centuries, who was appointed to the position of Junior King of Hungary. Gyula and Kende were Hungary's two leaders, with roots in pagan days. Gyula was the administrator and military leader, whilst Kende was the priest-witchdoctor-rainmaker.

Cseke is a remarkable graveyard. All the graves are marked with boats, boats destined to carry the dead to the next world. This is a tradition based on the fact that the neighbouring population, interred there, were fishermen by trade. Towering above the boats is the monument in memory of Ferenc Kölcsey, poet and correspondent of Zsigmond Kende. He is famous for writing the very patriotic national anthem beloved of all Hungarians.

Kölcsey and Gábor's great grandfather wrote to one another during the years 1832 to 1840, a time of great political change and upheaval. These letters, written between them, were based upon the fact that they were both men of huge patriotism and commitment to their country. They decided between them that, if Kölcsey went to Pozsony to represent Szatmár in the Hungarian parliament, Kende would keep an eye on the politician's estate. The thoughts of the two men were consequently recorded on paper, letters collected by Kende, and carefully kept for future generations. Sometime in the 1920s half the letters disappeared.

It was in 1942 that the Russian Army crossed the border into Hungary from the Ukraine. Gábor was eighteen at the time and had just gone to University. He studied economics, with the idea of entering the diplomatic service. Those were the days when, if a landowner had three sons, one became a soldier, one a farmer, and the third a diplomat! There was little choice in the matter.

Cégény was only about 60 kilometers from the border. Gábor was the only member of the family with his father in the house. Éva and Zsigi were in Budapest, and Gyorgy was in the Army, defending his country. Gyorgy had done well and was, at the age of 24, the youngest lieutenant in the Hungarian Army. Their mother had died a short while before of her long-term illness, multiple sclerosis. It was good that she had been relieved of her great suffering and was spared the inevitable eviction from her beloved home.

They could hear the Russian guns; the Germans were still in the village. All the big landowners in the area knew that they would now have to retreat. At the time communism was greatly feared by the noble classes. It was only a question of days, or even hours. The two Kendes knew that they would have to flee and tried to save a little. Family documents were thrust into boxes, silver and jewellery were walled up, and the rest, pictures, furniture stayed behind. Everything they saved was loaded onto carts and sent to Budapest. Some neighbours, the Bánffys, breeders of famous horses, came to ask Gábor to take some horses back with them, towards the Russian lines. Their reason for doing this quite escapes me, but he accepted the challenge, and, whilst his father borrowed a car from the head of the German division of the Army in Szatmár, he headed towards the Russians with five beautiful horses. Having completed his mission, Gábor found his way south to meet up with his father.

The Cégény estate had been in debt when Gábor's father inherited it, in the early 1920s. His father, Zsigmond, had been a free spender, but yes, the economic war also hit Hungary after the first World War. Despite all his difficulties my father-in-law took on a complete renovation of the house. Gyorgy felt that its modernisation was necessary. We still have the architectural drawings of a bold design, superimposed upon the old home. Although not today exactly as it was designed, it is beautiful still. It is a loving house, full of the atmosphere created by the family of Kende. It is not pretentious. On the contrary, it fits into its surroundings cosily and quietly, perfectly happy to adapt to being the orphanage it was when we were there, and, I am quite sure, to being whatever it is they have turned it into nowadays. The farm was in debt, and my father-in-law inherited not only the place and the payments due on his renovated house, but also his obligations to his two sisters. Penury and saving ruled the household. At times things were so bad that bailiffs would come to mark the furniture for collection, which is what happened on one occasion when they labelled the very chairs that the family were sitting upon. Gyorgy was determined to repay the bank, despite the inflation that had hit the country. The last act that he performed when the Russians were about to arrive was to go, with two suitcases filled with money to the bank to make his final payment. He was a man of pride, and, even if he had condemned his family to a life of difficulty, he would hand on his inheritance intact, without debts. As it happened this was good practice. His three children never desired foolish fopperies during their lifetimes and were able to tackle difficulties with some experience from their past. His sisters both married well, but retained all that was theirs by right of inheritance. Gyorgy, seeing the inheritance act whittling away the estates made a proviso in his will that the family fortunes would no longer be divided after his sons' deaths. Istvándi would go to Zsigi, the woodlands to Gyorgy, and Cégény to Gábor. Éva was to inherit all property that had belonged to their mother.

7

Leaving Cégény was for my father - in - law a wrench that tore at his heart. He went to his sister's house in Budapest. Gábor and he arrived in style, in a large German car, some silver pieces and precious family papers with them. On the way they called on acquaintances and friends, all of whom were anxious to know news of what was happening in the north. The novelty of telling and retelling their story must have been of some help. Gábor, at the age of 18, was very excited at the idea of change and a new life. Little did he know what changes lay ahead.

The Budapest they knew soon became a city of waiting, waiting for the Russians to arrive. There started a frenzy of parties and wild gaiety that presaged an inevitable conquest and loss. The Germans and the Regent conscripted every young man they could find, and Gábor found himself on the walls of the city with a box of grenades! Feebly he threw them in the general direction of the Russians. He thought that at least this was better than being with his father, who expected him to keep his head down writing and studying for his next examination.

As the Siege progressed it became more difficult to find food. At the time the main mode of transport was on horseback, and consequently the horses were being killed as the Russians continued their attack. Skirmishes in the streets for this godsend of meat were common. When you are starving you eat what you can. Amidst all the deprivation and starvation news came that young Gyorgy had been killed. He was shot by a sniper as he stepped out of his tent. I wonder if Gábor and his father would have been able to conjure up sufficient reality to be able to mourn a beloved brother and son. Living as they did, hungry and fearful, the shock of losing him must have been clouded by their ongoing needs, leaving them no time to indulge their grief.

Gábor became increasingly desperate to escape. Finally he found a friend who would tackle the exodus with him, and they found a possibility in the train to Vienna.

His friend was one of the Bánffy family from Transylvania. It was he whom Gábor had helped to return horses to his home, some months before.

The two friends crossed the border from Hungary to Austria in a coal-fired train, somehow hiding under the coal. Coming to a valley, still in Hungary, the train had to climb to the other side by means of its own momentum. Several times it would try to stagger up the other side, only to slide back again. Hidden in the coal, the two boys were swinging between Hungary and Austria! They risked imprisonment and even death if they were caught. Near the border a friend who had a farm in the area arrived with a pig. The pig was their bribe for the border inspector. He served his purpose very well! The denial of liberty to travel was to endure for many more years in Hungary and other Russian occupied Eastern European countries.

The eastern part of Austria at that time was still under Russian occupation. Their aim was to cross the Hungarian border in order to arrive at the American zone. Although they had left Communist Hungary, there was still danger in Austria. In Vienna they learnt that a small train would take them to the last station near Linz. From there it was only a few kilometres to the German border. Refugees usually found a guide at this point, to show the way to the Displaced Persons (DP) Camp. The snow was melting and the creeks ran roaring waters. Once they had to cross one of these rivers. They learnt never to walk on new snow because their tracks would show their direction. Crossing the border they cast their eyes on the little villages with their church steeples. It was around 7 a.m. when they arrived. People were going to Sunday Mass. Liberation came on a Sunday! The villagers told them how to get to the United Nations Relief Association (U.N.R.A) centre. At long last they had somewhere to go. Gábor stayed with a Hungarian family, in fact the Regent Horthy's family, in the village for a year until he got his Irish visa. Ireland had been neutral during the war and would be more likely to accept a Hungarian than countries such as England, France or the United States. Ireland did not easily accept refugees. Its laws made it difficult for foreigners to work, whilst demanding a five-year sojourn in the country to attain citizenship.

Gábor chose Ireland as his second country also because of a personal connection through the Horthy family with whom he was staying. They had two girls who had been brought up by an Irish girl from Limerick. Through this introduction, a great friendship developed. Another friend who helped enormously was an uncle of the girls. He liked to shoot on the Hörtobágy - he went there for geese. He had connections with many Hungarian families, but lived in County. Kerry. Another reason for Gábor's going to Ireland, and probably the most important, was his meeting with the Irish TD Brian Brady in Budapest. He it was who accompanied two and a half tons of food, which was a gift from the Irish people to the people of Hungary. This gesture and the connection with Brian Brady strengthened Gábor's resolve to go to Ireland. Hungary did not command much respect in the other English-speaking nations because of her partnership with Germany during the war.

Having said his farewells to his friends in Germany he left, travelling through Holland and England, where he met school and university pals. In England he stayed with Veronica and Michael Roberts. Veronica had been a friend of his family since his sister, Éva, was a girl. He arrived in Ireland on12th August, 1947

8

Gábor's arrival in Ireland was immediately celebrated by the Brady family. They took him to Donegal where he joined the men of the family on their daily visits to the pubs, the sea, and in their laments about the continuous rain that prohibited the making of hay. When the weather finally allowed the sun to shine, Gábor was all prepared to work. The family greeted him with picnic baskets and swimsuits. They had all agreed that it was far too good a day for work! Such was Gábor's initiation into farming Irish style in the late forties! The Bradys and their relations the Dardises were wonderful companions and friends to him during his first weeks and later, in Ireland. Dan Breen was another good friend at that time. He took Gábor electioneering in County Tipperary. This experience gave him a great insight into country life in this country.

Gábor found several jobs that were badly paid, grooming horses and riding out. He would have liked to have been a jockey but was too heavy and too tall. He was looked after by the Bellingham family in Dublin who introduced him to many people. Beecher and Sammy Somerville-Large were another couple who opened their doors to him. They had been to Budapest and knew something of what he had lost. Throughout his life Gábor always spoke of the generosity offered to him by Beecher and Sammy.

Gábor's lack of money was his biggest problem. Finally he found a well-paid job, digging a tunnel under the Liffey, a job that included "danger money". At long last he was away! At night he would change from his filthy work clothes into a dinner jacket, fetch his girl, and go to some hunt ball or dinner party. Here he had a surprise. In Hungary balls were private affairs, given in peoples' houses, in Ireland he found that he had to pay!

He did jobs in building and managed to have enough to enjoy himself.   Finally, however, he got the job of his dreams – in Goff's, the auctioneering firm selling horses.   Through this job he met people of his own kind – people involved in farming and the land.

This job was not only reasonably paid but it meant that Gábor found many friends in the same firm.   Head of Goff's at the time was Tim Vigors, brother to Pat who ran the Sugar Plantation – San Jacinto, in Peru.   About four years after his arrival in Dublin, Gábor was recommended by Tim to Pat as a likely successor to the latter in his job.   This possibility was music to Gábor's ears.   He had always wanted to go to South America. He had to wait another year in order to get Irish nationality, but then he was ready to go.

Gabor's first years on the plantation were dedicated to learning about his job.   He went through every section of the company, always dedicated to knowing as much as possible.   Naturally he enjoyed himself, too.   Teddy Lindsay became a great friend, and they traveled together into the mountains and the jungle. Another companion was Charles Skinner.   Gábor's trip home to Ireland went down the Amazon to Manaos, and from there to the Caribbean and was never to be forgotten.   Apart from an incident in British Guinana when his driver stole some gems that he had bought in Manaos he had a time which was both instructive and fun.   He visited sugar plantations, and was kindly treated by the various managers as he went.

9

The basic background of my husband remained throughout his life as his raison d'etre. By this I mean his devotion to the land and the administration of it. In choosing Ireland he chose a country whose people understood what emigration meant. He enjoyed Ireland but felt frustrated at the lack of employment in the country. He would have to go to South America to find a job that would pay him enough to settle down.

We did not meet for another four years. By then he had spent enough time as a bachelor in Peru to have had space in his house for a wife! We were ideally suited. His rather somber character was balanced by my laissez-faire attitude to worries and tribulations. He became for me a husband who would be my love and partner for the rest of his life. I learnt never to bear a grudge and to draw on my basic tranquility and sense of humour whenever I found myself floundering. Music always helped, and I heard it everywhere. The sound of the sea with its syncopated rhythm, sounds of leaves rustling, and the varying sounds of the wind are only a few examples of music that I hear. Cooking is another effect of music – high notes are in lemon juice, whilst an old-fashioned brown sauce reflects the very low sound produced by baritones! One could manufacture anything using ingredients this way!

If I was committed to him and loved him, both good and bad, he returned the compliment, sometimes in an extremely irritating way. He put me on a pedestal. He really did not know how to treat women otherwise. When I met his father and he explained that the family had always been dedicated to their women, I understood. This did not necessarily cover sexual fidelity! Reading Hungarian historical novels, I recognise Gábor in every character.

BOOK 3
AN ENCOUNTER
1956

Arenberg Strasse, Salzburg

Rosa with Count Botho Coreth outside the forest retreat

Austria - With Countess Marianne Coreth (Gábor's cousin)

Rosa and Gábor with Marianne Ergellet

Vienna - Count and Countess Spiegelfeld with Alfi and Rosa

With Doreen Morehead in London

Rosa and spinach in Paris

IO

In our tiny country people had not come across refugees before. Gábor looked foreign and was therefore somewhat suspect. It was thanks to only one or two introductions from Hungary that he was accepted into the society of people of his own kind. For us it was unlucky that, only a short while before our engagement, a little criminal from England with the name Sir Patrick Murphy had hoodwinked a girl of our acquaintance and stolen from her a huge amount of money. Gábor was in a difficult position as a result. He was seen as another fortune hunter. Proving them wrong became for me an aim to be achieved during our working lives.

Gábor and I met in the Shelbourne Hotel in Dublin. It was July, 1956. By chance I had flown from London the night before. My father had been at a meeting and had seats on an airplane leaving for Dublin. He persuaded me to take an early holiday and travel with him. Having arrived I was loath to go to bed, and phoned Reggie Roper, a great friend of mine, with the idea of spending a night on the town. In response he invited me to join him and a Hungarian friend for lunch. They planned to go to the races at the Phoenix Park afterwards.

Gábor had arrived from Peru via the Caribbean. In Peru he was assistant manager of a sugar plantation and he had just been appointed manager, starting in September. Marriage was on his mind as he left for his triennial leave of absence. His new job demanded more than just overseeing the plantation. It was to be more a way of life than just a job, and he was on the lookout for a suitable partner. Pat Vigors, from Tipperary, son of a well known breeder of horses, was the previous manager and had set an example of commitment that had to be emulated. As part of his training for management, Gábor had just spent a month looking at sugar plantations in Central America. Arriving in Ireland, he was warned by Reggie that I would join them for lunch.

Reggie was somewhat late and I was alone. I saw a group of friends at another table, but did not join them. Gábor was with them and noticed my arrival. His first impression was "bad legs" but otherwise okay. Typical of an animal breeder, he saw this at a glance. It puzzled me when I heard it later. I never thought of myself as being the possessor of bad legs. On seeing his, of course, I understood. He had the continentally coveted tiny ankles, beloved of the Victorian world. My legs are pretty well the same all the way down from the knees!

Reggie took us to Jammets, a restaurant reached through an alley off Grafton Street, or, more grandly, through the main doors on Nassau Street. It was there that I had been taken for my first restaurant meal in Dublin about two years before. A delicious pea soup was part of my memories. Reggie was his usual bantering self, and I rose to the occasion. Gábor was delighted. We set off to the races, full of good food and wine. All too soon the day ended, and I had to catch my train to Cork. They stood on the platform, waving and blowing kisses until I could no longer see them.

Gábor was in love and I was in regret. I never expected to see him again. A friend was on the train, and I remember confiding that it was always the best men who managed to disappear on the very day that one met them.

Arriving home to Cork I found Tony Mitchell waiting for me. A great pal of my childhood, he had left Ireland years before and gone to the States with his mother and family. We had kept up a correspondence, writing about our mutual love of sailing, and his of cars and carpentry. Now he was planning to become a priest and was hoping to spend some time with his old friends before following his vocation. It was tough on Tony that Gábor rang that evening. All conversation suddenly revolved around that phone call. Poor Tony was rather shelved when Gábor asked me to marry him. I am afraid that I demurred and took a couple of days to think about it. A few days later he had his answer, and I had sealed my fate! He came to visit my parents, and the Cork Show, and took me to a hunt ball. Possibly the best memory of that hunt ball was walking home from the city with Gábor. The dance lasted until dawn, and the walk through empty stretches of my childhood had a magical quality. It probably took nearly two hours as we walked arm in arm. He was staying on the other side of the river; I never found out how he got back to his lodgings.

We spoke unendingly about ourselves. I remember that he confessed his love for someone else, and my self-confidence was such that it did not matter. Although I would not brook another woman, I was quite certain that he would forget her in time. I was right.

That night was one of the happiest of my life, with Gábor in my beloved Cork. Cork has an ongoing love affair with its citizens, who, each and everyone, thinks of his love as being unique. It is only when one leaves "the holy ground" that one can share such feelings with another person from Cork. To share this with Gábor was a precursor of what he would be able to give me when we arrived in Peru. Naturally we spoke about Peru, and what our lives could be on the plantation. He painted a golden picture, a picture that was to be verified in a very short time. I was primed and ready to love the place, and the freedom of living in the countryside, was appealing. London had become a prison of endless buildings, and I was ready to leave. His language and his descriptive narration enchanted me A strong Hungarian accent revealed his huge understanding and vocabulary in the English language

Six weeks later we were married. Lovely wedding presents were packed and sent to our ship the *Reina del Pacifico,* in

Liverpool. My mother and father did us proud – vintage champagne, great food, and a kind priest all made for a delightful day. It was Elsie, in fact my stepmother, who did all the work, Gábor got very drunk, and Dad had to ring the stationmaster to ask him to hold the train to Dublin for us. Fortunately he did, and Reggie, our best man, and I bundled my drunken husband into his seat. He slept the whole way. I suppose that was the first time since we met that I had time to think. Three hours with a new husband who was comatose on the train, and not a regret in sight! It was unfortunate that an outbreak of polio in Cork had kept many of his friends away. However, despite doctors' advice, Beecher Somerville-Large, who had been incredibly kind to Gábor when he first arrived, braved the illness, and came to the wedding from his boat in West Cork. The Irvine sisters, with whom Gábor had had lodgings from 1947 until 1952, came as well. None of my Dublin friends came to see me wed, but the Cork friends were all there, plus many of my Cork/London friends. Dad spoke beautifully, and Mum looked really exhausted as we thanked her for putting on such a wonderful show with such little notice.

My introduction to what Gábor had of family was in Austria, during our honeymoon. From Brussels we took a very luxurious train, the Orient Express. Met in Linz by Marianne Coreth, I began to meet the relations. Photographs above show Botho, Marianne and Marianne Ergellet in Austria. They were all welcoming and kind. We stayed in a hotel with rooms framed in wood and bathrooms in the corridor. This was not unusual in 1956, in the days before the invention of the word "en suite"! Everything was incredibly clean.

We ate with the family. Marianne's mother and father lived with them. Her mother, Kati Hodossy, was Gábor's aunt. Marianne's husband, Botho, was there too. His mother was also there, but, because of her age, was so bent over that she could not communicate. Despite her obvious disability she spent all her time in the garden, weeding and planting. Alfie was Marianne's oldest son - he took charge of us, and gave us a most enjoyable stay. Waizenkirchen is a small village, sporting a massive castle that had been taken over during the war by the army. This was where the Coreths originally lived. The house they lived in during our stay and our subsequent visits used to be a farm house for the manager. It was charming, far nicer than the huge mass that it faced.

Thoughts about the difference between the treatment meted out after the war to those who remained under Russian domination and those in countries such as Austria and Italy inevitably surfaced as we wined and dined our way with the Coreth family. Gábor's father in Hungary had been deprived of everything - his livelihood, his home - and his family and was now living in a tiny hole in Budapest. Austrians, among them the Coreths, had fought side by side with the Germans in World War 11. They also aided the massacre of the Jews, as did the Hungarians, but it was only the Hungarians who were punished. To find a rational reason for this baffles the intellect.

We stayed for a couple of nights in a hunting lodge that they had in the forest nearby. Alfie came with us and made what he called Krambambulie. This was a drink made with Slivovitz (very strong) and sugar. You fill a wine glass with the spirit, and then put a match to it. A flame appears and you place a cube of sugar on a fork and hold it over the flame. The sugar melts into the alcohol, which changes the colour into caramel. Quite delicious and very intoxicating!

Another relation had a big party. She was Marianne Ergellet who had adopted Elizabeth Coreth, Marianne's daughter. This was because she had no children herself and she wanted to leave everything she had to Elizabeth. Marianne Ergellet lived in an enormous house in Salzburg. The party was in our honour and we were introduced to a lovely crowd of elegant people. I regretted my lack of German, but everyone seemed to speak English and always made sure that they spoke my language when I was

within hearing.   In 1956, after the isolation imposed by the
war, it was a new experience to be with such gracious people.
Simplicity at its most sophisticated was the impression that I
received.

Elizabeth became Mme. Firth, and we saw her only a few years
ago in her lovely mountain house. She married a man who
manufactured skiis near Salzburg. The Salzburg mansion was
divided into dwellings for different members of the family.
There was talk about selling it when we were last there thirteen
or fourteen years ago.

We went to Vienna, and, on the way, stopped at the castle of
Alfie's friends, the Spiegelfelds.   The old Countess looked like
a little doll. She spoke English with a pursed mouth and coyly
offered us a purple drink called "Parfait Amour".   She showed
the family pedigree that hung in the hall, and there they were,
the O'Donnells of the well - known Red Hugh family one of
the Wild Geese who left Ireland in 1607.   The family is rightly
proud of its kinship with Ireland, and it made me feel happy
that the O'Donnells found such a beautiful place in which to
live, albeit so far from Ireland.   I had never been to such a
place before.   The castle was ancient, built of stone.   We had
to mount deep steps to reach the drawing room.   It was warm
there with a typical Austrian stove, and several people waiting
for us. I can only remember the Countess – she was unforgetta-
ble with her dark dyed hair and her painted face.   She radiated
the last century as she greeted us with effusion.

Vienna was a blur of cafes and buildings, with an atmosphere of
great excitement. Alfie pointed to some Hungarian aristocrats
who gathered together every day, all deprived of their lands and
homes by the Russians. He offered to introduce Gábor, who
declined.   The reason became apparent during our marriage,
when he avoided such people.   He found them boring, with
very little conversation other than bemoaning all they had lost.

The Russians were the bugbears who had stolen from them everything they owned. Gábor's attitude was there was only one way to cope, and that was to work hard and regain what one could through one's own efforts, without continuously thinking of what had been lost.. This dilemma was completely new to me, not the fact of the Russian takeover, of course, but the effect. The war from which we in Ireland had been completely isolated had not only deprived a generation of my age of understanding, but also the real knowledge of its many consequences. In our late teens and early twenties we used to talk nights away speculating about Hitler and Stalin, playing with how it would be to be part of such regimes. Now the reality of the scars suffered by millions in the loss of their land and livelihood obfuscated dinner table chat. Listening became my brief. The understanding of my husband became a task of love.

Gábor's own life until then reflected his beliefs. He had arrived in Ireland with little else save the clothes on his back and £10 in his pocket. He counted himself as lucky. That was in 1947. Now he had a good job, a wife, and £3,000in his bank account! In 1956 it was a lot of money. We felt rich as we made our way back to London and Liverpool. My sister Ita and my father awaited us. A Hungarian school friend of Gábor's was also there, Robert Domjan, and Sandy Milne, a friend from Peru. So we had a goodly posse of people to bid us farewell as we waved from the *Reina del Pacifico*.

She was a fun ship with excellent food and great people. Only one disadvantage became apparent. The swimming pool was in the bowels of the ship. I think that I was the only one to use it as we reached hotter climes. It was dark and lonely, and I was a swimmer. The compromise became a shower. Poor Gábor fell sick of something undiagnosed. The doctor on board was really only there to enjoy the cruise, and spent hours discussing the illness with Gábor. We never discovered what it was, but his recovery happened before we reached the Caribbean. This was fortunate since this was to be the highlight of our trip!

Nassau, Trinidad, Venezuela, Jamaica, Columbia and Panama were hot, steamy and beautiful. In Bermuda we took a taxi and drove through plantations of flowers, bananas and sugar. The roads were dusty but the strong green of the leaves made a wonderful backdrop to the white houses along the way. A feeling of belonging became apparent, and Gábor's obvious joy in showing it all to me became infectious. A true farmer, he knew his plants, and, even if he did not, he asked our driver, whose expertise was that of taxi drivers all over the world. He knew the answer to every question! We had lunch in a hotel that looked over the bay on different levels. The bay was dotted with boats of every size that were anchored well apart, unlike the cumulative effect of a marina that is noticeable today. It, of course, has its own beauty, but, a block of boats, sounding like plucked strings, groaning all the while, can never be compared with the single boat riding at anchor. We sipped daiquiris followed by the fruits of the Bahamas, cool in air- conditioned bars.

Back on board we were sated with views, and happy to swop experiences with our friends. It took some time to arrive at our next port of call, Trinidad. They grow anthuriums in Trinidad. It seemed that the very fields were painted, - red and green – and with the white houses they seemed to represent the Hungarian flag. Gábor had been there before, on his trip home, and knew quite a lot about how they were cultivated. At the time, commonplace now, the flowers were flown to New York every day. Looking at the fields of red flowers it seemed incredible to think that they would grace the houses and hotels of New York within twenty four hours. We went to a beach that was a cove, ringed by cliffs, the sea blue as the sky, and the waves brilliantly white. A path led downwards and we flung off our clothes, ready to offer ourselves to nature and the sea. To this day, nearly fifty years on, that beach remains in my mind, and the pleasure it gave us all those years ago. Reluctantly we drove back to the ship, hoping to return some day.

Venezuela was politically upset at the time that we arrived. Leaving the ship, Gábor had all our papers and I went ahead. A soldier who was amongst several lining the way ashore, stepped forward, and, without demur, shoved a gun in my belly. It struck me as being an overreaction, but he may have asked for my papers, a request I would not have understood since I did not speak a word of Spanish. I carried my own papers from then on!

Caracas struck me as being a city of destruction and hills. The houses were on hills, and one could see scars on the hills, where more development would take place. Already Venezuela was suffering from a surfeit of cash – oil induced. We did not commit ourselves to a return visit, although this was the very place to which we would return six years later. By then our great friends, Pam and Ruly Knox had gone to live there.

Jamaica was to me the Caribbean. Nowhere else throbbed with the rhythm of steel drums with such verve and style. Walking in the street, with music blaring, people could not resist the compulsion to sway amongst the vegetables, the meat and the medicines. Fruit juices made on the spot, were from the Gods. A drive through the trees to the top of the mountains, soaring above their verdure introduced us to another taxi driver who was garrulous to the point of peril on the hazardous roads. Mysterious tales of voodoo and priests of a strange cult were not surprising in such a background. With the sea always in sight, our drive to the heights was exciting. It is a wonderful country.

The Panama Canal was an engineering feat, well recorded and amazing to go through. To be on a liner, kidnapped by the various locks and being taken from one ocean to another was quite an experience. It was calm between the locks and we sailed through leafy palms and bananas. Panama City showed little to passing liners, and it was here that we bought tax-free perfume that turned out to contain only water!

The Pacific heralded our arrival home. After a short while we crossed the equator. There was a good party to celebrate. I was lucky not to be dunked in the pool, since it was my first time over the equator, but the pool was too far away, thank God.

Callao is Peru's port. Here we had to say goodbye to all our Chilean friends, foremost of whom was an old gentleman called Chato Madge. He had accompanied us nearly everywhere, and we left him sadly with promises to meet again. It never happened. Such are the friendships made aboard ship. Chato had introduced me to the best of chivalry in South America. Again and again the caballeros of Peru reminded me of him. Darling Chato was in his 80's. It was wonderful to realise, early in our marriage, that Gábor and I valued the same people and to know that the friends that we would make in life need never bring controversy between us. This has been one of the great successes in our marriage, one that is essential in any relationship. We have shared our friends and, with very few exceptions, any friends we have had, have remained friends all our lives.

By now I had heard many aspects of Gábor's life. He was 33 and he was born on 26th March, 1924. He must have been a big baby because, to aid his birth, forceps were used. His right eye was damaged, and he was left with only five percent vision in that eye, but the other eye was good. His sight was never an obvious problem to him. To prove it I remember an evening in the Hotel Chimu in Chimbote. Instead of driving up to the door to collect us, he took off in the people van that we always travelled in, and started to circle around a flowerbed again and again! A mad moment that needed both eyes!

Well I must return to Callao. The first thing that I noticed was the rather ghastly smell. It permeated every corner "What is it?" I asked. It was guano – a famous fertilizer that is sent all over the world in a sanitized fashion. It comes from the islands off the Peruvian coast, islands where seabirds have been shitting

for generations.   It is a huge industry, with many men shovel-
ling and shunting the stuff on to waiting boats.   Strangely, after
some months the smell was no longer offensive.   Maybe it was
because, as Irish farmers say, "Where there is muck, there is
money."

We were met by Pat Vigors in the company car – a blue Chevrolet,
with its own driver, Wooton .   Wooton was shy and respect-
ful.   He put our cases in the car, well assisted by the stewards
from the boat.   In 1956 to travel was a delight.   Liners were
divided into three sections, 1st Class, 2nd, 3rd.   All the luxuries
that one can conceive were offered to the 1st Class passengers (I
had Russian Caviar every night for three weeks).   Sometimes
I wished that I could stay on the *Reina del Pacifico* forever,
round and round the world.   Actually some of the passengers
did nearly that – they boarded in Liverpool and did a round
trip!   They visited the various ports, but returned every evening
to the boat.

Reina del Pacifico, en route to Peru

Reina del Pacifico, en route to Peru

Teddy Lindsay and Gábor – with friends

BOOK 4
PERU
1952 - 1962

Rosa on Fosforito

Gábor speaking to workers

Transporting cane to factory

Gathering cane

Nepeña River

I I

In Lima we stayed in the Bolivar Hotel where I quickly learned that in Peru a smile is taken as an invitation and after a brief encounter with a lift-boy, I took care to be accompanied by Gábor or some friend at all times.   What a lovely hotel it was! Our room was huge and included a sitting room for entertaining.   The hall on the ground floor was so elegant that one had to straighten one's back and walk serenely!

We were due to go to San Jacinto after another day in the metropolis.   We saw the sights, and arranged to have our liftvan delivered.   That evening we went to a typical restaurant.   It was a fish soup, and I thought that my pallet would never survive the onslaught of chilli peppers!   This was my first taste of the famous Peruvian culinary art.   Lima was a surprise.   The architecture is baroque and flamboyant.   The streets are narrow and the pavements even more so.   Colourfully dressed people from the mountains sat on the ground selling their wares.   A great tradition of art pervaded their display – their industry apparent in the beautiful blankets and rugs made from llama and alpaca wool.   Vicuña was kept for the more opulent markets of Paris and New York.   Toys and trinkets made from silver were another treat, but it was the women themselves who caught my eye. They were clad in bodices and great voluminous skirts topped by panama hats.   They sat there silently, warm in their wool, a baby on their backs occasionally being swivelled round to a swollen breast.   They had a life of their own, placidly accepting the noise and intrusion of the modern world.   That placidity struck me immediately.   They were cholos from the mountains, but they had their own culture and never posed a threat.   Years later we were in Senegal and went to the market. How different the African vendors were!   There I felt quite frightened as they clawed at my clothes and tried to prevent my

passing without buying. South American Indians have a wonderful patience and acceptance of their lot. This has been well
documented, but the beauty they create with their handicraft
was a surprise for me.

How different were the rich of Lima. Wonderfully dressed
they used a lot of makeup. There seemed to be no connection
between such people and the Andean peasants. Occasionally
a wide setting of cheekbones betrayed some genetic link in the
past, but those who were well-to-do generally had European
features and height. In years to come I would discover that a
middle class hardly existed in Peru. What there was of it was so
small that manufacturers did not bother to produce plastic and
other cheap materials for the households. The rich imported
what they needed from abroad whilst the poor could not afford
to buy anything. A middle class is essential for any economy.
The moneyed class or oligarchy hold the country together until
it is upended by the onslaught of the new and educated middle
classes. Revolution has always been the result of education and
impatience. The latter is the child of the former. A thirst to
have "everything" at once is the aim of those who push towards
riches and success. Their creed is "you only live once."

Great exceptions prove the rule. I am thinking of those men
who helped build Ireland following the expulsion of the British.
It became obligatory for many to invest whatever profits they
made back into the country in which they made their fortunes,
in this case, Ireland. I never met a Peruvian millionaire who
did not have his money abroad, ensuring his living in case of
revolution.

We left Lima for the plantation less than a week after we arrived. A young Dutchman, Jan Esmeijer, travelled with us on
our journey. Wooton drove. We drove from the suburbs and
then past a new settlement, with houses made of reeds, constructed overnight by immigrants from the Andes. They were
there illegally, but there were so many of them that it was im-

possible to drive them away. They came quietly during the night and their neighbours awoke to find themselves in a town of straw having gone to bed in a wilderness! Just beyond these houses lay Ancon, the playground of the rich and beautiful. It is a country of the extreme always dramatic in its presentation, be it in its scenery or its people or its food. Suddenly we were in the desert. This desert lines the coast of the country and covers all terrain up to the mountains, with a few exceptions created by the twelve verdant valleys of which many were sugar plantations like San Jacinto. Signs of human habitation in centuries past, castles cast in adobe, demonstrate how the landscape has changed over the centuries. Paramonga is one such example, boasting an edifice fit for kings.

I found the desert exhilarating, but the Dutchman covered his eyes – he was miserable at having to live in such a place. Between us we exuded a very typical reaction; one in awe of the beauty of the country – the other totally in despair. Extremes are manifest in a totally exaggerated country. One felt the power of the place. One felt overcome at the majesty of it all and one felt very humble.

As we drove through the desert imaginary shapes appeared in the sand. They were honed by shadows. Grave sites could be noted by the telltale excavation marks. It was a custom of the cholos to venture forth on nights of full moon, to excavate the graves of their ancestors. Fortified by large bottles of Pisco, the Peruvian brandy, they went into the areas where the bodies lay. With a long metal rod, called a huaquero, they prodded the ground. If there was some resistance they dug, and lifted what they could from the grave. They showed little respect for their forebears as they discarded skulls and limbs They hoped to find gold or silver but mostly had to be content with ceramic pots of one sort or another. As I rode by an Indian settlement one day, I was lucky enough to rescue a lovely piece of carved wood from being used for firing. It has a face carved on top, with a base that must have been dug in as a marker in the sand. To this day it has pride of place in our house.

Twelve rivers traverse the coastal desert. Each of those valleys, made arable by the water, is home to sugar and other plantations. Of the larger sugar plantations, or haciendas, San Jacinto was the smallest. The largest, Casa Grande, was the size of Belgium, San Jacinto covered 42 square miles. About forty five minutes from Chimbote, the nearest town, my new home was situated at the foot of the Andes, covering all the land down to the sea. Alexander Selkirk's "I am Lord of all I survey, From the mountains right down to the sea", kept springing to mind as we drove up to our house – the Casa Hacienda, which was to be our home for the next six years.

Hills on both sides of the valley were maritime. Maritime hills are the geological debris left by volcanoes erupting under the sea. They are easily detected since one can gather sea shells right up to the summit of those small mountains. It is said that they blossom in times of rain, blossoms from the seed banks that have accumulated for centuries. One old man told me that, although beautiful, the flowers have a stench evocative of death and decay. When big rains come they flood everything. This happens every twenty-five years or so. When we arrived in 1956, it had been more than twenty-five years since the last inundation. The very road that we took up the valley was in fact the dry river bed that had been left by that iniquitous river called the Solivin. It was forbidden to touch, or change, the course of this dry river bed. It waited for the possibility of flood and preserved the path taken by the last floods in the 1920s. We were lucky never to see the Solivin in all the years that we were there. I remember seeing once a slight dampness in the river bed. That was all I saw. It was a different matter in 1968 when it arrived in all its filth, wreaking huge damage in its thunderous path, swallowing whole fields as it went. We had left in 1962, but we were devastated by the news of our beloved San Jacinto. Someone sent me a video of the horror of it all.

We reached San Jacinto. The journey had taken four and a half hours. Two large ficus trees hung over the space in front of the house. Well tended lawns were terraced and a large veranda with climbing plants adorned the house. Our quarters lay behind.

A dance had been organised to greet us on our first night. Present were all the senior employees and many of the others, factory workers and people from the hospital and schools. There were speeches and congratulations, presents and promises. Finally a huge bunch of flowers was presented to me. Not used to such treatment, I whispered to Gábor "what shall I do?" "Give her a kiss" he responded. It was exactly right, and I was into my new role.

Raol Dreyfus, John Baugh, Ted Kiendl with Sullivan
(my dog) The working life of San Jacinto

Lunch in Chimbote, Gábor speaking

Gábor visiting the kitchen staff

Factory Workers

Sugar Factory

Classroom in School.
Teacher is a de la Salle
brother

Fiestas Patrias, 28th July

Distributing Christmas gifts to the children

Janice and Gábor

The Lindsay family

Dancing La Marinera

Teddy, Janice and us

12

"San Jacinto llamando Lima, San Jacinto llamando Lima!!!!!!!!!", repeated again and again. This was the music of the office attached to our house in Peru. Radio communication was the only direct contact with the outside world. Our house was of one storey with high ceilings and dormer windows; it was an old monastery, built in the sixteenth century complete with church at one end. The monks were still there, buried under the floors of our rooms. The entrance to the cellar was located in front of the altar, marked by a large stone slab. We never felt the necessity to examine the area. Now all is gone, house and church, and the monks are lost forever under tons of rubble. The earthquake in 1968 made sure that we would never see our beloved house again. But in 1956 everything was in good order. We had a priest to say Mass, and servants to keep the house in impeccable condition.

Because we shared our living quarters with Gábor's offices, the house was approached by a hidden door, leading into a patio full of flowering bushes. Some of the offices, including the radio ("San Jacinto llamando Lima"), had a window looking onto the patio. Fortunately we had a drawing room and a sitting room, making it possible to preserve our privacy during the day. Our dining room presented no problems – it was adjacent to both rooms and could be used with either.

The radio call to Lima happened several times a day. Its installation was one of the innovations during Gábor's term of office, probably prompted by the strike that happened shortly after he took over the administration of the sugar plantation. San Jacinto was situated in the Nepeña valley and was 450 kilometers from Lima. There was little to draw one to the city. All one's daily needs were amply supplied by shops on the farm.

About four times a year I would go to Lima for necessities beyond the capacities of the local shopkeepers. There I would stay with friends such as the Knoxes, or, indeed, with Gerard and Gladys Lindsay. In later years the Sewells were kind enough as to put me up. All these people and many more used come to the farm, either on business or for breaks away from city life.

Pam Knox was one of the best friends I ever made. She introduced me to the joy of exchanged confidences, the analysis of one's inner self and the fun of false judgement on our peers! One of the very few tourist type journeys I made was with her to Huancayo. We stayed in a hotel (with Gábor it was nearly always a tent!). To be with a kindred soul in Huncayo, on top of the world, at Carnivales was splendid. Music, dancing and colour in that mountain town made us laugh and exclaim. There was a proliferation of native art, all with a very practical purpose. Crosses made of tin were highly decorated. They were made to be put on the gable end of houses in construction. These crosses were symbolic of an ancient placation to the Gods, due to be discarded on completion of the house. The air was thin and clear until a huge clap of thunder was followed by lightening.

My friend Pam was somewhat zany, loved to read and to laugh, and had a dachshund called Pully. Pully always came to stay with us when Ruly and Pam went away. He took over on arrival and bossed my much bigger dogs around the place in no uncertain manner. When we rode out on the farm he would struggle to keep up with us. He usually ended up in Gábor's arms. Pam and Ruly nearly always spent Christmas with us. They became our family abroad as we did the same for them. Unfortunately they left Peru, and apart from a brief encounter in Venezuela, our only contact until she died was by letter.

Gerard and Gladys Lindsay were parents to Teddy who was an agronomist on the farm and Gábor's companion on many trips into the jungle and the sierra. They were enormously kind to me when I broke my arm only weeks after arriving in San Jacinto. They lived in Lima and when my arm became infectious, they took me into their house for some weeks.

The Sewells were of the British Embassy. Tom had been given the post of second in command so that he would be on hand for Prince Philip's visit to the country. Jennifer who was born Sandeman of the famous Sherry family did not really like being away from her beloved home in Dorset. Eventually on her return to England she set up a wonderful dressage school on her farm. Her daughter carries on the good work today.

There was huge unrest in the village when Gábor acceded to his new job. The wise thing would have been to negotiate with the workers as soon as possible, but unknown to the workers, high-powered talks were going on between the English owners in London about the sale of the property to Americans, embodied in an Investment Company by the name of Wood Struthers. Gábor was firmly instructed by the Lockett family, the English owners, to cover things up, and to keep the peace until matters had been settled. Much against his will he had to ignore the pleas of the workers. In the meantime, negotiations carried on between Liverpool and New York. It took some weeks until all was resolved; and the very day subsequent to the final signing of the sale, the workers downed tools for the very first time in the life of the Company. By then they had unionised themselves Hotheads among the senior staff were keen to run the factory themselves with a few of the white-collared workers, but Gábor refused to sanction this, taking the view that there was present such unbridled fury, that such an action could result in bloodshed and even anarchy. They marched in their hundreds on our house. I was there with my broken arm. The more belligerent workers were in front, and Gábor was down the fields on his daily tour of inspection. Word was sent to him and he returned. Afterwards he told me that, as he drove through the crowd at the back, they made way for him, and greeted him with the greatest respect. "Buenos dias, Señor." He drove up to the verandah of our house and stood there, waiting for silence. I was out of sight to one side and never felt as proud as I did that day of him who was my husband, controlling and cajoling people for whom he felt such sympathy, people who had become the pawns of the powers in NEW YORK and LIVERPOOL. They dribbled away. This march on the house never happened again, not only because military commandos took up residence in front of our house for about three weeks, machine guns at the ready, but mostly because the people of San Jacinto were people of tolerance and trusted Gábor's words. The Guardia Civil on the verandah were boys, longing to hear the rat-tat-tat of their guns. They were there to defend us, but I was a lot more frightened of them than I was of the people. It was a bad time, but Gábor did not fail in his conciliatory attitude. The union was established, and the owners had to accept the fact that their autonomy had received a death blow. From that day forward the workers had a voice.

The strike was finally settled, and Gábor was left with the trade union, or sindicato. The leaders were people of little education; Gábor had to teach them all about running a sugar plantation, so that they could learn what rights they had. Like all unions in those days, the San Jacinto Sindicato was infiltrated by communists and other radicals. It had its funny side too. They presented their demands, and amongst many, they asked for two houses each, one for the wife, the other for the mistress! They were proud of the fact that both ladies had families. They became more wily and clever, and continued to be a thorn in Gábor's side for the rest of his tenure, but they never went on strike again in San Jacinto

One could not but feel great sympathy for the eruption of feeling in the strike, conscious as we were of how little the workers earned. It stayed with me, and, as we were going to New York to brief our new owners, I wondered in what way I could help Gábor and satisfy my own love for the San Jacinteños. It bothered me that most of the inhabitants depended completely on the Company. I saw this as being akin to Ireland's domination and patronisation by the Anglo-Irish, and previously by the English. Patronisation is an evil when the patron decides to go, leaving a big insecurity in the lives of their dependants. All the signs were that the owners in Peru, mostly foreigners, would soon have to pack their bags and leave. What would happen to the people then, used as they were to having someone else to help with their problems?

When they had come in anger to our house, I noticed that the most belligerent amongst them were the women, in particular one Señora Lostenau. I found out that she made tamales, a type of corn pancake stuffed with hard-boiled eggs and pork, for a living. I ordered some, and they were delicious. She created for me a lodestar in tamale-eating! Thinking about her, and her great voice, a germ of an idea came to me which was to become *El Club Social de Damas de San Jacinto*. The rest of my time on the plantation was to be devoted to this club. I formed a committee, which was composed of ladies from not only white but blue collars as well. We set about denoting our aims and inviting members to join us. The aim was to try and help others, and thereby learn how to help ourselves. We started by giving every child up to the age of 12 something to wear, sweetmeats to eat, and a toy at Christmas. This was quite an effort since there were at least two thousand children in that age group. We also tried to help the needy. We formed teams from the various neighbourhoods for volley ball and basketball. This created a great feeling of fellowship, and there was eventually great competition also between the barrios or suburbs. We took children on outings to the beach and other places. To make money for all these projects we ran dances, put on films, had American tea parties, competitions for sewing and baking and flower arrangements. It was democratic – anyone who wished to join could do so. The committee met once a week, and every week there was a gathering of the members, who had tea, followed by a lecture or a game of cards, or indeed a game of volleyball. We became good friends. We were the very first association in the valley to dedicate ourselves to the betterment of women and children. My main aim was to make people aware that they themselves could help themselves. I could see what might happen, and, above all, having been made aware of what Communism could do, I wanted to try and educate people into defending themselves against this atrocity. I knew that the land might be taken over, and, in my bones I could feel how easy it would be to impose Russian iniquity upon a credulous people. But it was imperative to do it the right way.

The population of San Jacinto was about 8,000. Amongst those were white collar workers, the men who worked in the offices and the factory in an elevated position. They were bookkeepers, engineers, mechanics. They were also schoolteachers, nurses, social workers. These were the educated people in San Jacinto, and they had the better houses in the village. The priest, for some reason, lived in the middle of the village. Perhaps it was because he had a wife and several children. He would normally have lived with the bachelors near the church. His family necessitated a bigger house. This was a very acceptable way for a priest to live, in Peru. I was somewhat surprised. I think it all came from an acceptance of sexual behaviour. What was wonderful about this acceptance was that even the educated people, albeit devout Catholics, had the capacity to understand basic human instincts, and the difficulties that they can bring about. Houses that were a little less comfortable were for the workers, who worked in the factory, in the fields, the garage, or indeed the hospital. Finally came the Indians. They were casual workers and they were housed in dormitories. They came as needed in lorries from the mountains. They were the recipients of gross injustice. Living in the Andes where there was no work, they bought their needs from shops who gave them credit, usually at inflated prices. When the work on the plantations needed them, the shopkeepers transported them down to the coast where they had the privilege of working off their debts. The shopkeepers took their wages. They were all addressed as "Cholo", had apparently no names, and spoke an entirely different language, Quechua. They came in groups for a short time and left for the mountains when they had finished their term. One story experienced by one of the field engineers was never explained to me. In the course of his work, one of the agronomists, Jorge Mongrut, was driving down a farm road when a large group of cholos came in view. He drove towards them, expecting them to get out of his way, but they did not. He kept on driving, and, at the last moment, the crowd parted in the middle. Right in front of his camionetta they had left a baby on the ground, ostensibly to be run over. Speaking about the incident some opined that they had proved themselves to be animals, but my shock could not be dissipated with European logic. Years later this sort of thing became very common in a movement led by Guzman, who led the movement called *"The Shining Path"* in the 1980s. Those poor wretched cholos were fooled into thinking that all their suffering came because of the presence of the gringo in the Andes. Many Europeans and Spanish-speaking Peruvians lost their lives. I am told that Guzman also became involved in illicit drug smuggling into other countries. After several years Guzman was captured and will spend the rest of his life on a guano island in the Pacific.

Perhaps now I should mention a book about the Andean Indian that was written by an Irish priest, Chris Conroy. Fr. Conroy lived with the Indians for several years and wrote about them with a sympathy that led to an ultimate despair. The book is called "A Beggar in Paradise, Living with the Inca Indians" (Mentor Press 1977). It is one of the saddest and true summation of a people lost in the sixteenth century, isolated by language and culture from the twentieth century. His extraordinary humanity as he strove to reach an understanding of the Indians was beautifully expressed in his book. One little story I found really evocative.

A little girl, ten years old, was suspected of stealing some money. He knew that if it was true it was because the little mite was hungry but he felt that he had to make her admit to the wrong she had committed in taking someone else's property. He called her into the house when he was eating his dinner and asked her if it was true. Noticing that she could not take her eyes off his plate, he realised that she was starving. Calling for another plate of food he shared his dinner with her for the rest of his stay in Peru. He finished that story with a declaration that he would not mind if she stole all the gold in the province.

There were about thirty professionals who lived on the same side of the Solivin as we did. The village lay on one side and the administrative offices, our house, the guest house, and about twenty other houses lay on the other. The village was above the river bed but otherwise quite flat. Everyone worked for the same Company – Negociacion Azucarera Nepeña. Our house was on the bottom slopes of the maritime mountains that surrounded the valley. There was a graveyard surrounded by high walls directly behind the Casa Hacienda. In it there were many people buried that had been taken from a foundered ship in the 1920s. They were mostly Scots with a few English names. Between the monks who were buried underneath us and these poor souls, we could never escape from eternity. Living there, between the Andes and the sea, one felt humble before nature in all its might.

Bertha, Hilda, and Jacques Vandergheim on the boat with us

Gabor with Queen of Fiesta

Goodbye Achu

Rosa in a canefield

Gábor on horseback

Bryan, Lorraine and Allison Lindsay,
Janice and Teddy's children

97

13

During his first few years in Peru, before we married, Gábor did his time as an apuntador. It was a job on horseback, a job overseeing all the field work in progress. It was standard practice to initiate the training of a future manager in this way. Through the overseeing of the daily work, he got to know the names and faces of all the stewards, something which was of enormous importance later on. Noting down the hours and work ongoing was strenuous, necessitating hours of paper work after supper. At that time, he was already living in the house that we would share. He employed a cook called Henriquetta. She terrified him. Janice Lindsay often told the story of an evening when she invited Gábor to dinner. He arrived complete with his own meal that Henriquetta had prepared for him before she left! He gave it to Janice to dispose of it! He did not want Henriquetta to know that he had not eaten it!

There is a wonderful tradition of cooking in Peru. As in France every region has its own dishes. The recipes come from ancient times as witnessed in the samples discovered again and again by archaeologists as they excavate graves. Maize is the ingredient that is found, food buried with the bodies to help them on their ways to the next world. Their precious objects were also with them – ceramic pots and objets d'art. Our kitchen became more Peruvian and more exciting as I settled in and discovered what Henriquetta was really capable of doing. Henriquetta was black, a great big woman who moved slowly. She was descended from slaves, imported from Africa. Hers was a great presence, as much mistress of the house as I was.

In the meantime the Americans were coming down to see their Peruvian property. Cuba had a sister plantation, owned by the same people. They were full of messianic zeal, ready to install a new factory for making chipboard out of sugarcane stalks and to build a new up - to- the- minute housing estate. Money was no object, and they took no heed of Gábor's warning of impending Communism, both in Cuba and Peru. They went ahead. A few years later it gave Gábor no pleasure to know that he had been right. I longed that we could own our own place, make our own mistakes, and enjoy our own successes. We had no children and no one to compromise but ourselves. But we had to stay, to make money, and to fulfill our contract. For me there was no hardship, and the irritants that Gábor had to put up with were not daily.

Gábor had settled in with the Americans very well. In particular, Ted Kiendl was a great addition to the San Jacinto team. He was Managing Director of the company in Lima and lived there with his wife, Elizabeth. Ted used the guest house whenever he came to the farm. He and Gábor had a great rapport and respect for one another. He did not throw his weight about, rather preferring to go with Gábor, respecting his experience.

Individually the Americans were charming. Two engineers, Tod and Hedeen became real friends, and kept us entertained nightly, drinking vast amounts of whisky. Ted and his wife, Elizabeth Kiendl, were a delight and they are friends to this day. Sam Milbank was the head man in the controlling company. He was odd, but entertained us regally when we went to New York. He took us, first of all, to a golf club on Long Island, and then to a house, a few miles away. This was his family home, large and dusty, obviously unused and unloved, where cobwebs obscured the dark paneling. He came from a well known, hugely rich family. His mother was a Borden, of fame in the milk industry. His apartment in New York was quite different. Here everything was spick and span. His wife, Molly, found it difficult to leave her yoga to entertain us. I heard later that she suffered greatly from depression. There were, of course, other Americans, but these mentioned were our closer friends.

The biggest shock came with the arrival of the Cubans. Our sister company in Cuba had been nationalised by Fidel Castro and, suddenly their top management was landed on us. They were bitter from their experiences and arrogant in a way that only Cubans can be. Amongst them was one good friend – a Dutchman from Indonesia, a brilliant chemist called Delden. He took no part in the politics created by his fellow men. The worst of them was a man called Scopetta. He was a fat legged man with a huge chip on his shoulder. He came from the worst element in Cuba and had married a very rich wife. His only wish in life was to regain what he had lost by annexing San Jacinto for himself. His means to this end was to create chaos out of the management team, without realising that without their dedication and knowledge, the entire structure could collapse.

Gábor's day began at 6 a.m. Sometimes he would go to where the field workers gathered for breakfast, followed by being transported to their respective fields. On one such occasion he was called to the bedside of an Indian who had stayed in bed, demanding to see the boss. The man lay completely covered by his poncho until Gábor arrived with an interpreter, who was also his driver.

"What is wrong, Cholito?"he asked the man
"Señor, every day when I wake in the mountains, my member is completely hard, but look at it, it is dead. I am sick, I must return to the mountains."

The poor little man was persuaded to go to work and gave no more problems.

There was a beautiful innocence and peace amongst the people of Peru. They were kind and looked after the frail amongst them. There was no need for orphanages nor for old peoples' homes. Those who had to be looked after mentally stayed in the villages and were called the loved ones of God. Within our village a certain pecking order prevailed. Gábor was, of course, at the top, and, as his wife, I was "*la primera dama!*" For some reason no other wife had ever become as much part of the village as I had. For this the people were enormously grateful and showed their gratitude in huge demonstrations of fireworks and festivals on my birthdays. It was all very embarrassing.

I enjoyed driving around the farm with Gábor. Irrigation was of supreme importance in such a dry climate. Great reservoirs were fed by the yearly inflow from the only river. It was thanks to this river that the plantation existed at all. The water was captured and sufficed for the coming year, for the people and for the crops. Pockets of underground catchment areas augmented the supply and in total made of San Jacinto Jimbe, Moro, Motocachy, and all the other villages a verdant, prosperous place.

There was also cotton growing. It was wonderful to see the cotton piled up in sheds, whiter than the whitened walls. Fields grew liberal amounts, and the pickers raced through the job. But, of course, sugar cane was the principal crop. There were no seasons in growing cane. In one day it was possible to see the sowing, the growing and the harvesting. To start a field of cane a young field had to be cut and laid out ready for splitting into even lengths. These lengths were lain evenly in trenches on the ground, fed from a tractor by two men. The cane grew until it flowered. It was then set alight and burnt. The sugar of course prevented the total extinction of the plants. The burning merely got rid of all the leaves and the weeds. The Indians, or cholitos from the mountains then entered the cooled, burnt fields, and cut the cane, which was laid in neat bundles in a convenient place. It was convenient for the huge tractors and trailers, or the company train, to take to the factory that worked day and night, extracting sugar. This was done first of all by crushing the cane, extracting the juice which was then centrifugally made into crude sugar. Finally the sugar was bagged and taken to the port, and shipped to God knows where.

There was a herd of Friesian cows on the farm. They produced enough milk for everyone. Milked by hand, it was fun to watch what happened. Seated on milking stools, the men called out the name of every cow in turn to come and be milked. The cows knew their places, and waited patiently for the summons. I would have spent more time with them, but the flies were dreadful; it seemed amazing how the men tolerated them.

We spent many hours in Motocachy. On a hill it was slightly cooler than anywhere else in summer. It was there that grapes were grown, primarily to make Pisco, which is a 1st distillation brandy. It has become well know as one of the best of such brandies in the country. I suppose that it was there that I grew to love all white spirits, the crudest that are produced in every place. Not for me the Napoleons etc.!! Motocachy was lovely with acres of vines, avocados and other fruit trees. We loved to go there and whenever we had guests, it was one of our first ports of call   Aresse was the farm manager in Motocachy. He shared my love of dogs and willingly undertook to help me with one of them. Silky had a skin disease, and it was recommended that she should swim in the sea every day. At the time we were going on leave for three months, and, of everyone in the plantation, I asked Aresse to help. The poor little animal had hardly any hair left. Three months later I returned to a fully recovered Silky with a lovely new coat.

The higher employees lived in an area called Solidex. There was my greatest friend, Janice Lindsay, and her husband Teddy. Most days I would potter down to the Solidex for an hour or two with Janice. There was a huge swimming pool, of regulation size, at our disposal. Over the years Janice and I raced one another, sunbathed, tried to swim a kilometer every day. There was also a tennis court of which we made full use. We played whist, canasta and backgammon. We kept busy, and were able, at the same time to look after her two children. Those were good days. Teddy, Janice's husband, had been on several trips with Gábor before we married. They had crossed the Andes behind us into the Callejon de Huaylas. Teddy and Gábor were very close friends and remained so all the time we were there.

The Salazars, the Hoseas, and the Mejias were other families in the Solidex. Julio Salazar was head of the offices and a lawyer in his own right. Hilda was a great worker in the *Club de Damas*, and a dear friend of mine. The Salazar's niece, Bertha Usquiano, became very special. She helped enormously with the club, but was almost a liaison contact for me with the happenings on the farm. It was from her that we heard of peoples' difficulties, outside the usual channels.

Every night Gábor would sit in his office until about 10 p.m. if necessary, waiting for anyone in the village to come looking for help. He never spoke to me about their problems, but, sometimes, he would give money to our club in order to help difficult cases. Bertha was a great help. I credit her with teaching me Spanish, albeit with a northern accent! Bertha still visits us on a pretty regular basis. She helped look after Daisy for a year from seven to fourteen months. Now she relishes Daisy's children, and wishes she could see them more often.

The Mejias, Dora and Gaston, were another couple in the Solidex. Gaston was head of the garage. Sometimes we had dinner together. One evening, with them, I learnt a lesson about what not to do in Peru. There was a jug on their table, the like of which I had not seen before. It had a special tube of glass for ice down the centre. I admired it, perhaps a little too much. At the end of the evening, figure my embarrassment when the jug, beautifully wrapped, was presented to me as a gift! I was careful not to make the same mistake again. They were a lovely couple – she also helped with the club, - and he was a top class man in charge of the garage. The garage maintained all the trucks, tractors and probably even the trains.

The Hoseas were David and Marjorie, and their daughter, Jeanie. David was the accountant on the farm. He was Scottish and Marjorie was English. Marjorie was a good friend and also helped a lot with the Club. Her daughter was a very clever little girl, and Marjorie taught her her first years of Primary School. Later a special teacher was brought in for the children of the altos empleados (the top employees). Because we had no children we had no needs in this direction. The lady who filled this job was bilingual and her name was Esperansa Allemandt. She came from Lima, and stayed, happily, for many years in San Jacinto. The Hoseas often gave good parties, in particular at Christmas.

Johnnie and Bessie Boyle were also Scottish. He was an engineer in charge of the factory. He had strange fantasies at times, sometimes accusing Gábor of not being Hungarian, or late at night, dancing naked on the lawn in front of his house. Bessie was also quite amusing. She stomped into Gábor's office one day with her ration of meat. She threw it on his desk, asking what animal would eat such a thing. It came as a great surprise to him, as he called for a cloth to mop up the blood, because he presumed that the butcher apportioned the ration on a fair basis. His solution was to exchange her ration for ours.

Some of the Europeans had difficulty with the local food. Gábor and I really loved it, and in my kitchen, our laundry woman reigned. She collected recipes, and was a good cook. Her name was Delia, and she had a daughter Olivia. Olivia had a baby out of wedlock, and Delia was somewhat upset, or pretended to be – this was a very normal happening in San Jacinto. When I asked how the baby was doing, Delia told me that she never looked at the little one but that, if she passed through a room where the infant was, the baby's eyes followed her all the way! Delia was a great help over the years in finding new and good ways of cooking. Her laundering was top class too, albeit all done in cold water, with a washboard.

Road to Huari

Andean village, Huari

Going to Lapra with a mule train.
Lapra is part of San Jacinto but in the Andes

Picnicing in Lapra

A typical café in the countryside

Looking back at the Cordillera Blanca

We met this man as we left Pomabamba

Cold

Harvesting in the Sierra

Beautiful Indian girl with her daughter

Gossiping the day away!

Local child

14

One day when I was preparing to go to Lima to hear and see Michael Mac Liamoir in his production of "I Must be Talking to my Friends", Gábor suddenly appeared with news that we were about to go on a trip to somewhere called Pomabamba. I couldn't believe it – I had bought my ticket months before and longed to see the production. He insisted, I demurred, but not for long. Instead of a suitcase I packed a saddle bag, and we set off for the Callejon de Huaylas, with Achu, Gábor's driver. For the first and only time the car broke down on the summit. We were there for nearly two hours. Eventually, Achu figured out what was wrong, and we set off for Huaraz, which we could see below us at a distance. The plan was that we were to have dinner with the man who was to be our guide to Pomabamba. His wife had a delicious spread waiting for us, and we were hungry! Having eaten my fill I suddenly had to vomit, rushed to the lavatory, managing to throw up everything just in time. Everyone knew what was wrong. I was suffering from soroche, or mountain sickness, the result of having spent too long at high altitude.

Making apologies, we left our hosts and went to our hotel. I fell fast asleep, but, on awakening felt really hungry again, and ate my second dinner of the day. In the morning we went to see an outdoor museum, housing the collection of a priest. It was superb. There were hundreds of stone statues laid out on paths, decorated with flowers. This man truly loved his archaeological pieces. I sincerely hope that his exhibition still exists.

Soon it was time to go and find our guide, who was waiting with our horses. There followed an easy day's ride across the plains of the Sierra Blanca, so called because the peaks were always covered in snow. The Andes that we could see from the farm were called the Sierra Negra, i.e. black, because those peaks never had snow. Lovely photographs in slides show us resting on the slopes, with a mist shrouding riders and horses. It was a day of peace and discovery. A young and lovely pair greeted us in the next village. An Andean village like this had very few inhabitants, with houses built around a large square. Their little holdings were far away from the village, necessitating a very early start to reach their fields.

The evening before, we were taken to a room with a comfortable bed and a window overlooking the square. Asking for the loo, to my horror, I was shown into a shed piled high with compost. As I performed, I heard a few grunts, and realized that I was sharing my comfort with two fat pigs, waiting for my contribution! It was good to return to Gábor and my bed.

Next day we started at dawn, lovely scenes of harvesting greeted us as we rode. The corn was corralled in a circle, and with the aid of horses, mules or cattle tied to a centre pole the grain was separated from the straw by their walking feet. Whilst this was happening, a band played huainos or, occasionally, marineros. Echoing through the mountains it had a strange, haunting sound. The bright gold of the corn, the black horses and the colourful garb of the Indians enhanced the beauty of our going. Similar scenes awaited us as we rode. Wild flowers, such as lupins, and a narrow track were relentlessly leading us to our next adventure We saw it before we approached, a black hill looming ahead. It did not look promising. Our guide was certain that our path lay across it. We had to take his word – we had no other.

The path led forward and we followed. It was a hill of flaking slate, taking us higher up the steep conical hill. My mule was surefooted and unafraid, but it took a great effort on my part not to feel frightened. Every step the animal took loosened the slate path and sent bits of slate tumbling down the precipice below. We could not ride abreast, the path was so narrow.

Looking back, I could see my poor man absolutely scared and preoccupied for me. He advised me to be ready to throw myself towards the black hill if the mule decided to fall. It took us fourteen hours to reach our destination – a trip that should only have taken three. The people of Pomabamba had gone home, and we had to find a place to stay. It was our first wedding anniversary. The very simple hotel had one narrow bed in a room already occupied by twelve people, all male! It did not matter. Exhausted, nothing stopped us sleeping that night! Next day there were great celebrations when our hosts found us! I was escorted to a lovely, airy room, complete with chamber pot, and snuggled down for a few hours.

Gábor had business, but came to call me in the afternoon. Although completely isolated, Pomabamba is a charming little village. I particularly remember the sound of flowing water. Drinking this mountain water was an experience never to be forgotten. It was like drinking liquid silver.

That night we were invited to dinner. Somehow the ladies of Pomabamba had not consulted between themselves, and four of them had prepared veritable feasts! The solution was to present them all together, and make us eat the lot!

Nobody warned us!

Course after delicious course appeared! I gave up after three, but Gábor carried on valiantly, eating ten of the twenty four courses! What an experience it was – Peruvians considered it bad manners not to partake of everything, but they were gentle with us, understanding what had happened on our journey! They also explained that we had been guided onto the wrong road. The road we took was a worn old path that had not been used since the time of the Incas – not since the sixteenth century.

We set off for home the following day. I was sorry to say good-bye to my mule, as I greeted a rather fat grey horse for the final lag of our journey. Following the stream we came upon a big and beautifully-kept holding, boasting an unusually large house. We were still miles from civilization. Invited in by the owner, we were shown into a high-ceilinged room with walls covered in the most lovely old wallpaper. Astonished, we asked from where it had come, and how. By ship from England and then on a mule train from the coast! Further delights greeted us such as housed sheep and a perfect loo in a little cabin situated over a flowing stream!

Two photographs taken by Gábor on the path we took on our way to meet Achu remain for me to be typical of the Andes. The first is an old man, so lined that there is little else on his beautiful face, with eyes of sadness. The other is of a young girl, spinning as she walked. Dignity and poise are the themes of this photo. For centuries those people have worked and suffered – they have been encouraged to chew cocaine, encouraged so that they would not suffer from hunger, or from cold. Coca was grown deliberately so that the Cholitos would never complain about their miserable lot. It was sanctioned by the government when we were there.

Our trip was coming to an end, we were shortly to meet Achu. He was there. As usual he had a story for us. Across the valley, on the other side, he pointed out a group of houses. He told us that the people who lived there had a cure for cancer, known only to them – a special herb. One could go there and be cured. It was a fitting end to a wonderful trip. I read recently about a Shaman type of cure that is advertised for tourists. It may be the same.

15

Back in San Jacinto we bathed and dressed, and ate delicious home-cooked food. To feel clean is a luxury. Warm water caressing one's body is one of civilisation's greatest gifts. The quenching of thirst with cold water is another. To be alive and full of joy can be achieved with the happiness based on the mutual love of two people. Gábor and I were lucky in love and in the enjoyment of living together. Ireland was very far away as we entered our second year of marriage. How laughable were the doubts of my relations as I appreciated every day of living with a man of substance, no longer the refugee but the very best of all the men I had met in Ireland and England.

People from the States and Cuba constantly visited us. We had a guest house that was beautifully run by a man and his wife. They would stay there, and we would have them come to dinner with us during their stay, as many times as they needed. In the 1950s it was all quite formal, - not dinner jackets, but definitely dark suits. I had quite a collection of fairly glamorous dresses to wear. During the day I wore jeans and a blouse. Dr. de la Riva, who was our consultant doctor always criticized me for letting down my title! Gábor dressed in cream coloured slacks, with a shirt, topped by a panama hat. The mounted senior staff wore these hats and with wear they acquired an individuality. We wives could recognize our husbands from a distance as they rode towards us, from the shape of their hats. Most of the field work was done on horseback.

Nearly every day I used go to the stables where my horse would be waiting. In the winter, from May until August, I needed a cardigan for about an hour; after that the cardigan settled around my waist. Getting to know the farm this way was great. Our visiting friends often joined me. On flat land one could spend hours on horseback, rocking to the pace of these

Peruvian horses. They are small, with an amazing ability to carry big men and heavy loads for extremely long hours. This was the only way to explore the archaeology of the place.

One of the first things that one observed were the Incaic waterways. They indicated that in times before the arrival of the Spaniards, there were many more hundreds of acres cultivated. Footpaths connected valley to valley. The people themselves were the beasts of burden since they had no horses. If the evolution of birds was proved in Galapagos, knowing their history, the Andean cholo was the same. His short but strong body, perfect for lifting and carrying, was held together by sturdy, short legs. I have seen them, when we were puffing and panting, walk straight up the side of a mountain. Surely their ancestors' lifestyle had something to do with their shape. Our modern life that does not involve much lifting or carrying has produced the tall long-legged people, first encountered in Germany and in Sweden.

16

Every three years Gábor's contract specified that he had to return to Europe for three months.   This had something to do with the old Colonial dread of their employees "going native". Nonetheless, a fully paid vacation was appreciated   It was called "going on leave".

We flew over the Brazilian/Peruvian jungle to get to Rio, on the first leg of our journey.   It was before the advent of jet planes, and, as a result, we were able to realise how huge a space was taken up by those trees.   Once again I was made conscious of the difference between a view and the experience.   Being in the jungle was an enveloping memory – viewing it from on high was to see it all quite differently.   Perhaps had we never been there, we would never have been able to imagine what it was, from the tops of trees!   As it was, it was like trying to see through a window with closed curtains.   Our journey seemed to go on forever, with a sea of green below.

Finally the huge statue of Jesus heralded our arrival at Rio airport.   Situated between two hills it was a steep descent to our destination.   We were taken to our hotel, the Excelsior, and immediately felt the strangeness of a new country.   The full sight of Copa Cabana lay just outside our window.   We went out immediately.   It was delightful to see so many beautiful women walking about, bikini clad, doing their daily business, shopping etc.!   It is probably difficult to imagine why I was so surprised at seeing so much flesh in 1959, but in Peru the Spanish idea of extreme modesty still prevailed at that time.   It took me no time to emulate them, (not in a bikini, but a swimsuit), and to join in the excitement of being close to the most fabulous beach, probably in the world.   Gábor followed suit, ready to enjoy the sun.   We lay on towels because the sand was full of tiny animals that tickled the skin. When we could no longer bear the heat, the sea was there to refresh us. A long walk followed, and finally the best Sangria Tropical we had ever had, in the hotel. News awaited us. Our flight, scheduled for the next day, was cancelled. We could wait for the plane to be fixed or we could take a flight with another company. All inconvenience would be covered by the airline. Of course we opted to stay. We had to stay in Rio for a full week! We walked all over the city and took a taxi to the Botanic gardens. Rio de Janeiro is a place of constant delight, interspersed with horror. Poverty was so obvious there that one's inadequacy in its face was in truth crippling. There had been poverty in Peru also, but it had not reared its head quite so obviously. Cities are cruel places but they beckon to the needy because of the riches of a few. What the rich throw away waits for scavenging.

The Botanic gardens were, in fact, full of trees from the Amazonian jungle. What a joy it was to walk through. Gábor took photographs and we felt lucky in having such a marvellous time, thanks to Air France. We had some money in Switzerland and the bank accommodated us with transfers.

A funny happening was one chap's way of getting to meet girls on the beach. He had two miniature poodles on a lead; he had trained them to lick a sunbathers ears. It was most effective, the girls immediately jumped up and received effusive apologies. What a game to play! I could only be flattered when my ears were assaulted!

The day came when the plane was fixed, and we were on our way to Africa. There were only four passengers, and, of course, the crew. It turned into a champagne party flying across the Atlantic. We all travelled first class and we got to know one another really well, in a fairly inebriated fashion. Arriving in Senegal, we discovered that it was a bank holiday in Africa, and the hotel was full – we had lost our bookings through staying in Rio. Our new friends, the air hostesses, doubled up in one of the crew's rooms, and gave us the other. On waking next day, we found a vista that was, for all the world, like a painting come to life. A glittering sea lapped a sandy beach, which was populated with tall, black, elegant people either in or about their boats. An inviting thatched cabaña was serving drinks to people from the hotel. We joined them for a while. The hotel was built by the famous French architect, Corbusier, and he had made use of every stone to add to the natural beauty of the place.

Our main purpose in going to Senegal had been to travel to Timbuctoo but unfortunately it was not possible because the river was dry. Instead, we decided to visit the building that had been built as a holding place for slaves on their way to America. Seeing that place was one of the saddest things we ever did. Even the walls screamed the agony of the poor souls, who had been dragged from their homes, disgorged into this horrible place, and then transported by slave ship to unknown destinations. There was even a hole in a wall through which anyone that died was thrown into the sea. It is terrible to witness to what depths we humans can fall.

From Senegal we went to Paris to meet Gábor's sister and her husband. This was my first encounter with another member of the Kende family. She was full of questions and kindness. Her husband was in the Swiss diplomatic service, and they had recently returned from India. Their flat was near the Bois de Boulogne, and it was there that we played with their three children, two boys and a girl, Isobel, Peter and George Éva and Richard showed us their Paris and even had a cocktail party in our honour. We left for Ireland after a few days, promising to get together again during our leave. That promise was fulfilled due to the generosity of my parents. The Pestalozzis joined us in Currabinny where Mum and Dad had a summer house. We shared the cooking and housework. Éva was astonished to see me using a cook book. She hadn't realised that I never had to cook in Peru. It was just as well – I didn't have a clue, and had every confidence in Delia who did the cooking. We explored Cork, we sailed, and we were invited to peoples' houses. It was a good time, a time that made up for the years of enforced separation between Gábor and Éva. We tried to go to Hungary, but the "Iron Curtain" still enforced complete isolation on its inhabitants, and gave no quarter to intending visitors. Visas were insisted upon but not given.

It was a lovely holiday. We enjoyed Currabinny and the woods. A few days before we left for Peru, a directive arrived from the holding company of San Jacinto, telling us to change our flights to America and to go instead to California to look at citrus growing. This was indeed a surprise. We flew to Los Angeles and then took a bus to Santa Barbara, a delightful Columbian town. My sister Ita was in San Francisco, and came down with Gábor's friend, Sandy Milne, to meet us in our little hotel.

Eating grapefruit from the trees was a new experience. New sweet varieties had just come to fruit. Everything we saw was wonderfully kept, and Gábor agreed with his new owners that Peru, and Motocachy, would be a good home for citrus. We also saw some lovely Aberdeen Angus cattle grazing on what seemed to be bare hills. But no. A completely dry clover (burr clover) was their sustenance. They had shiny coats and plenty of meat. This is veritably a miracle crop!

It was a pleasure also to meet Elizabeth Kiendl's parents. They were Prince and Princess Poniatowski, descended from the last King of Poland. They showed us everything, including their lovely colonial house, but, best of all, introduced us to any farmers of interest in the neighbourhood.

Meeting Ita was really nice. She had settled into her job as Assistant Matron in a University Hospital, It was only a few days, but we managed to catch up on our lives, with great promises of writing more often. In later years, she deeply regretted not having come down to Peru.

Too soon we had to leave, and we took a plane to South America that would stop for a few hours in Mexico City. Those few hours gave us a top-class taxi driver who took us to see the architecture of the city. Nationalistic, colourful, gigantic were the words that jumped into our minds. Mexico City is redolent of a fierce reaction to the United States. It is no wonder that there are so many border issues between the two countries! The history of the Aztecs is one of might and violence, and the people are proud of it. Paintings of enormous size, depicting their past, copying the past, cover modern buildings. They are determined to keep all this alive.

Gábor's hunting companion

We did have some luxury holidays too!
This one in Senegal

Senegal

Gábor with hens

Rosa waiting in canoe

Suburbs of Iquitos

Banda de Yumpa

124

Our makeshift home for a couple of weeks

Amazonian house

17

Back in San Jacinto it was not long before another trip was planned to Tarapoto in the heart of the Amazonian Seco Montaña or dry jungle. Tarapoto is a village and it was here that we bought some land, never registered, but with serious intent. The hotel was one to dream of. Thatched with palms, with all bedrooms leading on to cool patios, it was one of the best hotels we had ever stayed in The only fellow guest we came in contact with was a General in the Peruvian army who was very self-important. Speaking of his great accomplishments in the war against Bolivia or Chile, I teased him by asking if he used a blow-gun!!! In the evening we went to the cinema and were vastly amused by the reaction of the audience when, on screen, they saw snakes and monkeys, something they met every day in their own lives. Maybe it was the music that made them frightened and caused the screams of horror!

On the following day we went up river in a dugout canoe. We passed salt mines on the way and several rafts carrying cargo. These were made of bamboo and constructed to fit the load. If an animal was on board, the raft had a leafy roof of palm. We saw every conceivable type of cargo on the river. On going ashore for refreshment in a village, suddenly the entire population rushed towards us. We couldn't understand, but found out that they had been waiting for some politician. We were sorry to disappoint them, and carried on up river.

Gábor had organised in advance some horses for the next leg of our journey. We had eaten heart of palm in the hotel the night before, and the chaps who brought the horses offered immediately to fetch some for us. A tree was felled, and the heart was proffered – an enormous helping – enough for a week. On horseback we traveled for half a day until we reached an idyllic spot, a clearing beside a sweetly flowing river. Gábor built a shelter that was to be our home for the next two weeks. I had brought a book with me and Gábor had a gun. His plan was to shoot a jaguar whilst mine was to read and float on our lovely river. Happy days they were with Gábor returning every day before sundown. Across the river there was an Amazonian family. I used go and visit them on occasion. One evening one of them came from a different direction. She was very agitated. She told me that there was a girl further up the river, delivering a baby. The girl was in dreadful pain. Would I by any chance have an aspirin? I gave her six, - she told me that it was enough. Next morning she returned and told me that the baby had been born and that the girl was very grateful for the aspirin. She sent six eggs to me. What power an aspirin has!

Those days of peace and loveliness have remained with me as a paradigm of the retreat needed within one's life. Totally re-moved from ordinary living, Gábor and I knew that what we were experiencing would be difficult to replicate ever again. One night, when Gábor had not returned, and I was dozing in the tent, a most extraordinary noise woke me. It was some-thing that sounded like a cross between a screech and a ghost. Terrified, I listened, but, although the noise seemed to come nearer, it always retreated before coming closer again. Gábor's return made enough noise to frighten the creature away. We found out later that it was a prehistoric bird, a survival from the age of the dinosaur, a big bird with claws on its wings. The hoatzin is about 25.6 inches long but weighs less than a kilo. It has a long tail and may have lived 36 million years ago, dur-ing the Eocene Epoch. Predators such as tayras and capuchin monkeys provoke a response of hissing, hooting and yelping. The hoatzin nest over water and when attacked, the young dive into the water, regaining afterwards their home by means of the claws.

....

Fascinated by the lovely place we had been to, we returned to a similar place. To get there we had to go to Buena Vista. Teddy Lindsay had a small holding at the mouth of the Rio Biabo. We flew to Buena Vista in a small plane with no seats, surrounded by Indians with chickens and their belongings wrapped in leaves. Gábor remembered a time when, traveling like this, the plane started to wobble provoking a panic on board, far more frightening than the fate of the plane!

A boat was waiting for us to cross the Yucayali river. The inevitable horses stood on the other side. They in turn took us to the Biabo, where canoes crossed to Teddy's place. The horses swam, with us leading them from the canoes. Teddy's little house was lovely, and well equipped. His man, Constancia, looked after us exceedingly well. The following day we set out to the head waters of the Biabo, going as far as possible on horseback.

As we rode up river, at first the land was all being prepared for agriculture. A few brave men like Teddy Lindsay had put their money into the dry jungle, so called because it had less rainfall than the Amazonian delta which was surrounded by swamps and areas impossible to cultivate. Teddy's farm was gradually being cleared of trees in the traditional way, first by burning and then by time and rain. As we progressed along the river little holdings boasted vegetables, chickens and pigs. It was hot in the saddle and we stopped, not only to give the horses a drink, but a swim also. We all got in – horses and people. It was there that we found our canoe, a really big one. The horses could go no further, gone were the small signs of cultivation, and we set out, paddling. I trailed an arm in the river. Suddenly our guide and paddler raised a long stick that he had, raised it high and crashed it in the water near my arm. A huge snake came to the surface, dead as a dodo. He had spotted me from a tree on the shore, saw a tasty meal, and, like lightning, made for it. Am I glad still to have my arm, all because of that little man!

We arrived at our destination after about three hours in the boat. Now we had even run out of water! No more horses, no more boats – from now on it was shank's mare! Gábor's longing to shoot a jaguar was still burning. I had no such ambition, and was glad to remain in the little settlement until he returned. I hated to walk in the jungle, constantly falling over tree trunks, leaves and twigs, fearing snakes and other animals. Gábor loved it. He had flat feet, and this may have aided him, giving him a remarkable steadiness. He set off with about three or more men. They marched towards known jaquar spots for six or seven days, eating food they had brought along and cooking what they shot on the way. They had no luck, despite the expertise of his guides. Ten days after they left they arrived back to the settlement, finding as they returned that a jaguar had followed them the whole way!!

In the meantime I had had a brilliant time, reading, swimming and chatting to the people. In the house where I stayed there were about seven people and a little girl of about ten. The seven were the family, and they were industrious to the last. We all slept in a lovely airy thatched room. There were no windows, but plenty of openings to give a current of air. I had a makeshift chair on which I sat to read, during the day. The woman of the house, who felt that I was in her care, kept admonishing me not to read so much or I would damage my eyes. Swimming was lovely, just like a pool, - there was no current or flow, with plenty of depth.

The mother was fun to watch, during the day. She made marvelous food. One dish I particularly remember, chicken with groundnuts. She boiled the chicken, ground the nuts that had been grown locally, and then united them both with some additions, including coconut milk. This was served with rice.

On the way home, having arrived back in Buena Vista, we met the pilot of our plane. We had dinner together, and, hearing that we came from a farm he presented me with a monkey. It had been abandoned by its mother.   I took it and cuddled it, but found it to be utterly untrainable when I got home.   It broke everything in our sitting room and terrified our guests as it took leaps to land on their heads!!   I had to give him away!

18

Shortly after our arrival in1956, I acquired my very first puppies. Crosses between an alsatian bitch and a greyhound dog, they were christened Sindy and Cato. They were to become my constant companions during my six-year stay in Peru. Sindy was elegant, a well-covered greyhound, and Cato was black and almost terrier- like. Once they grew they became very protective, sometimes to my detriment. During an English class one of my pupils came towards me. Imagine my horror when Sindy, who was lying at my feet, leapt up and went for the jugular. Another time, someone approached me as we were both walking by the hospital, and, once again my faithful friend attempted the same defensive attack.

There are many stories that I could tell about my canine friends. Work on the farm started at 5 a.m. The dogs went for a drive down the farm nearly every day, jumping on to the small camionettas/pick-up trucks driven by senior staff members. Their journey often took them an hour away from our house. I was told that, at a certain point, they would jump down from the truck, and make for the Casa Hacienda where we lived. Both dogs would greet me as I left my bedroom. Every morning their rapture was apparent.

They were bred by the Lindsays, Janice and Teddy, and, when we left Peru, in 1962, we gave Sindy back to them. He had never lost touch with them, but, unfortunately, he never settled down to their ways. Whilst they were moving from one farm to another, - a distance of about 100 kilometers, - he jumped from the truck to the road and was lost. Months later, Janice visited the market in Casa Grande, the largest sugar plantation in Peru, and who was there but Sindy, far from home, bedraggled and woefully thin. Her joy was immense as she brought him home to a feed, a bath and a big welcome. They took him to Lima, but his lack of freedom killed him. Locked in the house one day, he went straight through the glass of a closed window on the second floor. He did not survive for very long. Cato went to another family and lived out his days quite happily.

I used to ride out nearly every day with the dogs. The first two were joined by two lovely pointers, Silky and Sullivan, named after the winner of the Kentucky Derby in 1958. It was a splendid thing, to be mounted in that beautiful country, surrounded by my hounds, and escorted by a stable lad.

When the dogs were still too young to follow me, shortly after my arrival, I took a tumble and managed to break my arm in two places. We were quite a distance from the village and the stables. There were some Indians working in a field nearby. The lad with me called to them to come and look after me, while he went for help. I lay there, very weak, in pain, comforted by people who only spoke Quechua, murmuring in exactly the right tones of sympathy. Quechua is one of the fourteen original languages, unadulterated by any other.

Indians from the Andes, colourfully dressed, and I was at one with them in a way that I had never felt before with complete strangers. By sitting on the ground behind me, they made a support for me with their backs. What they were saying, I have no idea, but I have always believed that I was destined to fall that day, to meet those kindly souls and to understand always a little of their humanity. Of course the stable lad was originally of the same background, spoke some of their language, and had given them instructions on what to do, but to this day I know that the Andean Indian knows more about the essence of things than I do. They generated in me a respect that I will always have and a gratitude for what they did for me during some hours of waiting. Like us all they varied in their approach to others, but it was their spirituality and their ability to accept me so readily into their group, quietly saying "mamasita" amongst many indecipherable words. I never knew who they were, but that did not matter. They would not have treated me in the same way ever again. They would have found even my gratitude strange. The money Gábor gave them was enough. For me it was a humbling lesson.

The plantation had its own hospital, to which I was taken when I broke my arm. The doctor at the time was a Lebanese/Peruvian, who used the farm to practice surgery; his patients all seemed to need appendices operations for one week, next week there was a proliferation of gall bladder removals, and so on. As the Administrator's wife I was sent to Lima for repairs. Unfortunately after the operation I developed an infection in or around the bone. That is how I came to be with Teddy Linsay's parents for several weeks. The arm necessitated daily visits to the hospital in Lima.

Gladys and Gerard Lindsay treated me like a daughter. It was in that house that I learnt to appreciate cooking and sewing. Neither art had interested me in the past. The sheer contentment of Gladys in being in her house was also an inspiration. It was lucky that I never felt homesick in South America. Typically Irish, I knew how to emigrate. Gladys and Gerard were also immigrants, but they were from a different time. Gladys was the granddaughter of Germans.

19

Gábor's contract was coming to an end and decisions had to be made. A Cuban called Scopetta helped us to make up our minds. He was an unattractive sort for whom Gábor had no sympathy. Strangely enough, since our marriage, there was nobody else for whom he had such disdain. It would have been impossible for Gábor to work with him. There was no way that he would have renewed his contract. If the Cubans had all been like our friend, Edward Delden – a great sugar engineer who had worked in Indonesia and Cuba, it might have been a different matter

Having made up our minds, vacillating between an offer to manage a sugar plantation in Mozambique or to return to Ireland, we decided to hit the tourist trail in Peru. Cuzco is in the mountains, and is the most wonderful Incaic city. The stone walls are made of enormous slabs transported from great distances. The Indians are at home in Cuzco in a way that they are in no place on the coast. Traces of their history can be found engraved in stone. I remember a place of judgement where an ancient groove, of no great depth, snaked down a large rock, dividing in two on its way. Where guilt or innocence could only be assessed by the Gods, liquid (possibly blood) would make the decision. Poured into the channel a man's future would depend on which course it followed. If it took one way the man was guilty, the other course set him free.

The Incaic throne lies in Sachahuyman in the neighbouring countryside. Massive stones impress, no doubt with intent. Was this place a place of worship, worship of the sun, perhaps? Whatever it was in ancient times, it continues to impress. Gigantic stones are in a semi-circle around an open, flat space. Maybe this used to be filled by an army of peasants. There are no decipherable records to tell us how this great place was used. There was only one little boy, all dressed up in his gala clothes, there. He was hoping for tourists, but only we arrived.

Ollaytaytambo was our next port of call. This is a fortress that guarded the valley from intruders from the west. Nowadays it gives one the opportunity to survey the beauty of one's surroundings. It is built to a great height, giving a superior view of the river that gushes through the mountains. This is the very river that leads to Macchu Pichu. What struck us most of all was the stonework everywhere. This was obviously to combat the rain and snow that are prevalent in the mountain areas. We were used to seeing wonderful structures on the coast, made of adobe. But on to Macchu Pichu!

We took a train from Cuzco, down the valley, accompanied all the while by the rushing river. Arriving at a little station, we mounted a bus that took us up the white, snake-like road all the way to the tiny hotel. This was in 1962 and like all the tourist hotels in the country where we stayed, our accommodation was comfortable and simple. There was another gringo couple staying and we arranged to walk to the ruins together next day. The term "gringo" describes anyone with white skin from another country. The people in the hotel were German and became good companions during our short stay.

The first thing I learnt about the magnificent pile that was Macchu Pichu was that all the bones interred there were female, which led people to believe that it was a sanctuary of women, gathered together for worship. The terraces that front it were for growing vegetables. A big mystery surrounds the high spot - an "altar" that is strangely and evocatively shaped. Below it is a hole containing water – it is meant to be the bathing place for the inhabitants. A mountain peak to the east was used for growing potatoes. It is astonishing that all these things were happening then, before the arrival of the Spaniards. It is astonishing to think that they did so without the benefit of the wheel. I was intrigued by the path left by Hiram Bingham (the American anthropologist who discovered Macchu Pichu). He had done all he could but left a slightly disguised path leading east from the ruins, for anyone who might attempt more excavations. In the evening we walked, or rather slid, down to the station and found our way to back to Cuzco.

Our next trip took us to Arequippa. Unlike Cuzco, Arequippa is a colonial city, baroque and beautiful. Like many similar towns the first impression is of whiteness. Once again the hotel was superb – this time in a more sophisticated sense, and Gábor was delighted to find that the manager and his wife were Hungarian. We walked around and enjoyed seeing the volcano in a grumbling state. It was the Misti of course. We had dinner with our new friends that evening. I found amusing the use of our three languages. I am quite certain that if I had spoken Hungarian, there would have been no need for English and Spanish. Gábor and the others kept slipping back into their own language, especially when the wine was flowing freely.

On the following day we took the train to Pisac. The landscape was fairly desolate, and, apart from a few herds of llama and alpaca, there was little to see. What made up for this was the train we were on. It was sheer luxury. Waiters in white gloves served food fit for the gods and wine from Chile. Starched white tablecloths, with silver cutlery and cut glass were all out of the last century. It was easy to relax and not to feel the hours it took to get to our destination!

Pisac and Lake Titicaca are another facet of the multi-faceted country of Peru. It was from Lake Titicaca that the Incas came. They suddenly shot out of the water and proceeded to make the country their own. They were white with red beards, making those of us who are Irish claim them as our own! The lake has islands that float, islands on which people live. It is the biggest lake in the world, and, annoyingly, Bolivia claims much of it. Pisac is full of vendors of everything Indian, giving the place a very colourful aspect.   Unfortunately we were unable to stay very long; we had to rush home for all the parties and fiestas in our honour.

20

The welcome we received in San Jacinto heralded the start of a series of parties and fiestas unlike any we had seen before. We were due to leave the valley in three weeks, and every single person wanted to say goodbye. It was overwhelming. Bertha Usquiano kept a calendar of events. As time went on even breakfast meetings had to be attended! There was no break and no time for reflection.

We watched football matches. We watched volleyball. We danced nearly every night. Fireworks and bar-b-ques, visits to neighbouring villages, all accompanied by toasts to Peru, to us, to Ireland, and whatever! Gábor had stag evenings too, from which he returned pretty legless. I had my womens' gatherings, arising from the *Club de Damas*. We were exhausted when, finally, the last day came and we were to be the godparents to the wedding of Gábor's secretary, Manuella Aguirre. It was lovely to see her, dressed beautifully, very nervous. The wedding party that followed signaled the beginning of our packing for the boat and home.

Finding homes for my dogs was difficult, but saying goodbye was worse. It became a debate as to whether one should have such faithful friends at all, if one knew that it couldn't last. My wild dogs would never have survived in a European country, all hedged in and small.

The spontaneous love and generosity of the people of San Jacinto, Moro, etc., was a huge tribute to the time when Gábor was Administrator. They also showed gratitude to me for my work in the *Club de Damas*. Gábor's integrity and easy relationship with the people was his achievement. His humanity was shown when the time came for Christmas bonuses.

Because of a loss, the company decided that there was no money for workers' bonuses, but that management would receive their due. This enraged Gábor to such an extent that he gave all his bonus to the men.

Driving through the well-known fields down to the Pan-American highway, it was like being sucked away – such was the love we felt for that life we were leaving behind.

Photographs taken on board the *Reina del Mar* show Bertha Usquiano, Julio and Hilda Salazar, Pat and John Baugh, the Kiendls, Jacques Vandergheim, - they were all there to wish us farewell. With great sadness we turned to our new life, secure in the fact that we shared the same aim; a farm in Ireland

BOOK 5
IRELAND 1962

Gábor with champion Bull, 1972

21

To leave Peru was to leave one's soul. They made parties for our going, just as they had done all those years ago for our arrival. Presents were showered upon us, presents that made sure that our house would always be Peruvian. To this day we love everything and enjoy the memories that all our memorabilia provoke. A picture of San Jacinto, painted by the American artist Brockie Stevenson, hangs on one wall, whilst pride of place is given, over the fireplace, to his painting of the first monastery founded by the Spaniards in the sixteenth century. Peruvians are extraordinarily artistic – paintings, sculptures, pots, and incredible weaving all show them to be talented and imaginative. Their music is a delight. To this day nobody knows from where the native Peruvians came but wherever it was, they arrived on the American Continent centuries before the Spanish. The Conquistadores when they saw land in America were convinced that they had sailed around the world and had arrived in India. This is why the cholitos, as the indigenous Peruvians are still called, are known as Indians to this day. The Spanish had no idea at first that they had discovered the New World. One of our pictures is a religious depiction of the Virgin Mary that is representative of the Cuzco School of Painting. Noticing the artistic talent amongst the "Indians", the Spanish used them to paint pictures for their churches. It is interesting to note that although the figures always wear European dress they have distinctly Indian faces!

It would have been exciting to have taken a return route to Ireland that would have introduced us to the Far East and Africa, but Gábor had no intention of abandoning our luggage. So it was heigh-ho to the liner *Reina del Mar*, the successor to the *Reina del Pacifico*. A more modern ship than her predecessor, she had a good sized swimming pool on deck, and plenty of deck chairs with a bar. We were not the only retiring plantation people. In Costa Rica we were joined by several Dutch engineers and their wives. They spent their time drinking their difficulties away and wondering about their future. I enjoyed one little episode immensely. There had been a storm all evening – all passengers sliding to their tables for dinner. Clutching to hand rails we found our way to the deck. The crew had emptied the pool, leaving a small amount of water at the bottom. It was inviting! The mad Dutch led the way, followed by an equally mad Irish woman. The ship heaved and leapt through the waves, whilst we were flung about willy nilly, all self control gone, in the swimming pool! Gábor was far too sensible for this frolic!

One of the main reasons for this exodus of sugar experts was the fact that Europe and the States had taken up the cultivation of sugar beet, thus wrecking the market for cane production. Peru faced decades of deprivation, brought about not only by market forces but also by the influence of Castro and his merry men. Communism became the cry of the day, and many landowners and business-men suddenly had to depart. It was chaotic in any case, but, on top of everything else, an enormous earthquake in 1968, followed by floods and devastation, hit our old home and valley. San Jacinteños born and bred had to upsticks and go to the States. For a people who loved their land this was heart breaking. Not too many people were killed in the earthquake, but to the best of my knowledge at least three of our friends died. Huge damage was done to the houses, including the old (sixteenth century.) house in which we had lived. Never again will we visit the place in which we were so happy.

News of such disasters reached us in County Kildare. It seemed unbelievable that the country that we had loved so much had had to suffer such losses. Teddy Lindsay and others collected clothes and other necessities to fill a couple of lorries in Lima, items that were gratefully received by the people of San Jacinto. There was little else one could do apart from organising field kitchens and so forth.

As one exists, it takes time to adjust to differing circumstances. The greatest inhibitor is oneself; does one take oneself with one, or, indeed, can one leave oneself behind? To travel, as we did, always brought the question as to how we could live under the same circumstances as that lived by the people we were visiting. This question has no validity, of course, but we had to knuckle down to a very different way of life when we bought our farm in Ireland. It was hard to think that all we had known in South America had virtually disappeared.

From the time that I left Ireland early in the 1950s, it had always been my firm resolution never to set foot in my native country again. Peru had solidified my terror of narrowminds, in that its open spaces and the familiar distance created by a code of behaviour that was never intrusive was always reassuring to my own basic shyness. Being no longer Rosa Doyle from Cork, but "Rosa Doyle de Kende", was not only the result of marriage but also the beginning of a glorious new freedom. I flew from Cork, I flew from London, but was rescued into a new life by Gábor. That was the best decision that I ever made in my life. I felt that everything would be negated by stepping backwards.

Of course this was a very suspect conclusion. From where I stand now in 2009 we did the right thing. Peru has never resolved its problems, and emigration has become a necessity for nearly every progressive youngster in San Jacinto. Another great earthquake killed hundreds in Ica only a few years ago There is a terrible expectation and acceptance of disaster in the mind of the Indian. This comes from the certainty of pending starvation, hunger and the difficulties attached to surviving at all.

Because of the work I did in the *Club de Damas* I was asked recently what my thoughts were on charitable activities in the "third world". It must be different everywhere, but when asked I had to reply that as long as people wanted you to help, it is easy. Certainly the San Jacinteños welcomed all we tried to do, and it was democratic in that everyone, and by that I mean not only the better off, helped.   There were no distinctions between people.   I cannot think how it must be when even your presence is suspect.   Pictures of starving children in Africa that are shown continuously on the television are becoming photo opportunities for the rich and famous.   Redolent of fairy tales of "The Beauty and The Beast" the glamorous pose gracefully, cuddling children with distended stomachs.   This last is probably an unfair comment, but it is all based on the "good feel" factor in one's being that is essential to all humans although denied to the destitute.   Again and again I have seen money splashed at poverty when in reality it might be more appropriate to try and become one with those one tries to help.

Before returning to our story I would like to say that I do not have the slightest idea about how to tackle all the crippling poverty in the world.   Perhaps historians will help, and maybe the coming climate change will turn countries south of the equator into new civilisations, who worry about how to help us in northern areas!

Our house in 1962

Another view of the house in Newtown Donore

22

Everything that comes
Goes and comes again
And our first glory returns
And the grown man does
As he did when a child,
There is no fate but the renewal of youth
Sean O'Riordain,Linte Liambo.

Presentiments and perceptions abound in this life but events recur despite them. Thus it was that I found myself once again in the land of my birth. Gone was the liberty of being unknown and my inevitable fate was upon me. The strangeness of Gábor's physiognomy allowed him to retain his privacy and authority. His very presence awarded him much respect.

What we found on arrival in Ireland was a reluctance to employ Gábor in the sugar industry despite his years of service. It was carefully explained to him that he could not be put into a position of due importance because of the numbers of people already in the company who might be offended by his employment. Length of service should be the only criteria for elevation in a company. The man in charge, a Mr. Costelloe, told him that he was exactly what they needed, but he was very sorry not to give him a job since his hands were tied! The question of the Irish language was also given as an excuse. The fact that Gábor spoke German, French, Spanish and English was of no importance when he lacked the native, dead, idiom! Such was the way the country was run in 1962! The sugar industry was a state industry in Ireland. Gábor tried other possibilities but came up against the same resistance every time.

All the pettiness of my own country was being demonstrated as we wasted our time on interviews. Gábor was more patient than I. Willing to keep on trying he kept signing up for more possibilities. In the meantime we spent a great deal of time looking for a farm to buy. Salvation came in the person of Bob Jeffers. A long time friend, he had found a farm near his place. He was the manager of Blackhall Stud, and had gone to buy hay from this particular farm. His description of cows with udders like tanks, and hay that had never been adulterated by artificial fertiliser was so enticing that we went to see the farm in Newtown Donore on the following day. Reggie Roper, our solicitor and mentor came with us. It took no less than a few hours to complete the deal, and our future was decided.

The farm was a delight. A beautifully kept farm yard led to fields in divisions of small paddocks all the way up to one field of 36 acres. The majority were around 11 acres. Altogether they added up to 133 acres. The fields were clean, - very little ragwort and docks. The land was flat - ideal for dairy cows. We had just enough money to buy the place, the papers were free of mortgage or other debts and soon we were the owners of what would be the most generous farm in the county. A year or two later we bought seventeen and a half acres on the other side of the road, which brought our holding up to 150 a.

We moved in on 1st September, 1962. One of the previous owner's sons, Joe, helped us initially, and without difficulty we hired several men to milk the thirty-five cows that we had inherited. We were used to the slower pace of life in the tropics, and so the Irish found us to be crazy, employing six men to milk 35 cows! They prepared to watch our demise and failure. They were right. It did not take long for us to realise that we could not afford to pay so many and in fact, after their first curiosity had been satisfied, the men began to drift away. It was a time of great unemployment, and the average man had become used to his bed, and found the idea of a very early start to be repulsive. The norm at that time was to be without money, meet your friends every evening at the Cock Bridge (only half mile from us), and drink your problems away. The Cock Bridge straddles the Grand Canal. This canal was built in the late eighteenth century. with the purpose of connecting Dublin with the west. Robertstown is only three miles from us and is the highest point on the waterway. There is a feed of water, the Milltown feed, that comes from as far away as the town of Kildare, flowing into the locks in Robertstown and filling the canal both on the side that goes to Dublin and on the other side to the west. It also creates another canal, that flows to the River Barrow, thus making a connection with Waterford, having joined up with the Rivers Suir and Nore. The fen from where this water came is very near Kildare, and when a new motorway was discussed it was neighbours of ours, Tommy and Charlotte O'Connell who were amongst those who fought to save the Pollardstown Fen from the fate that threatened the entire waterway infrastructure. By disturbing and "developing" the fen, the entire Canal system would have been at risk. Tommy and Charlotte saved a very important heritage.

....

My sister Ita had married just a few months before we bought our farm. She and her husband James helped us greatly, and told us about James' brother Peter who was in farming, with a great knowledge of cows. Peter joined us, and became the backbone of our existence for the first few months. He had an uncanny empathy for cows; he could smell out a sick animal from a group of 100 without difficulty. Little by little we learnt his skills, but it took many months.

There came a day in 1963 when we received word from Gábor's father that he had permission to leave Budapest for two weeks. His visa only covered Austria. His plan was to stay with the Coreths in Waizenkirchen, hoping that we would be able to join him there. After eighteen years of separation it seemed unbelievable that father and son would be united again. Gábor was delirious with anticipation, nervously looking over all that we would need, presents we would take, and any paper work that would be needed. I had never seen him so excited.

My father-in-law had had a very special relationship with his youngest son. The family place was designated to be Gábor's inheritance, hence father and son had spent many hours together riding and driving through the land that would demand a deep commitment to the best use of their place, the repayment of the huge debt that was owed, to say nothing of the care that they owed to their workers, and the village. As it turned out, with the advent of the Russians Gábor never took over the running of Cégény, but the training he had received from his father stood him in good stead for the rest of his life.

The great day finally came when we arrived in Waizenkirchen. He was a dapper little man, in appearance much younger than his years, and ready to have a good time savouring the delights of a comfortable home. The Coreths were enormously hospitable and actually left us alone with Gyorgi's sister Katineni for nearly the entire time. She it was who cooked for us and made the most delicious food, as excited as we were to be with her brother. To experience joy such as we knew it then was almost worth the separation that they had endured for so long. Naturally that is not true. Never would it be possible to make up for the years without family both for my father-in-law and for Gábor, the little things embracing what living is about, the sharing of difficulties and achievements. He had been a strict father but the certainty of his love had never been in question.

We retraced our steps when we visited the hut in the forest. It was there that we had sipped Krambambulie all those years ago on our honeymoon. We walked and we ate poppy seed cake. His English was poor so Gábor had to do a lot of translating. He was able to read English though and asked me to lend him a book, which he read aloud in a very strong voice. In this way the days flew by until he had to go. Familiar tears accompanied our farewells as he boarded the train that would take him to Budapest.

When Gábor's father died a few months later in 1963, it was Ita and James who came down to Donore to take care of any eventuality that might occur whilst we flew to London. For some reason the Russian occupied Hungary gave visas to those who had to bury parents. There was no embassy in Dublin making it necessary to go to London. From London we flew to Brussels where we boarded a train for Vienna. There was no air communication between the West and the countries behind the Iron Curtain. Another train took us from Vienna to Budapest. Eventually we arrived and had a happy reunion with Zsigi and Madi, Richard and Éva.

Immediately we set to finding out what we had to do. As it happened it took longer than we thought. First of all it took a long time to find the body, going from one mortuary to another. The Communist hierarchy enjoyed not helping us in our quest. Reams of paper work produced repetitive negation of my father-in-law's very existence. Finally he was found and we were able to bury him. Afterwards we were caught by one of the coldest spells of weather that affected all our travel plans. We missed every connection; both train and plane, and finally had to spend a night in Brussels. We were happy in the knowledge that Ita and James were in our place. It was our good fortune that no matter where we landed Gábor and I always seemed to have Hungarian friends in the area who would give us a bed. In Brussels it was the Jekeys. He was a very old friend of Gábor's. He came from a village only a few miles from Cégény. They had not seen one another for years. We spent a pleasant evening with them and were glad to find a plane ready to fly next day.

Apart from the fact that our inherited cart horse killed one of the cows by chasing her around the fields, all went well! That same horse was only used when the tractor would not start. The true meaning of horsepower was demonstrated as he pulled the little tractor around the yard! It is only from a distance that we seem to have been primitive – horses pulling tractors was a very acceptable idea in those days!

Possibly the greatest difficulty we had at the beginning was that of cleanliness. There was no running water on the place and no electricity to install it. A dear friend, Peter Simpson gave us the present of a hip bath. We put it in the kitchen, relying on the Aga to keep us warm whilst undressing. We had an anthracite Aga for cooking. It had a temperamental attitude towards its constant use. It had to be filled by coal scuttle twice a day, more when needed. This was Nancy's job. Nancy came to us just days after we had arrived and took on as her own, our lives. She was our servant, our family, and our friend. Everything that happened was as much her concern as ours. She was still with us thirty-five years later.

We had bought our farm for £10,000, representing all that we had saved in Peru. The stock was bought with the help of the bank. In all we started out in debt to the tune of £25,000. It was frightening in a time when our sole income was £200 a month for the milk we produced, and with this we had to feed the cows, pay labour, and try to feed and clothe ourselves. From the day we took over the place the cows, all thirty-five of them, started to calve, one after the other. Of course we lost some calves and suffered hugely from each loss. Gábor was waiting for an animal to start calving on one occasion, whilst I grabbed a moment to go shopping. On my way I saw a magpie, an ominous sign. In despair I turned round to go home, to acquaint Gábor of the news. His reaction was forceful, "This time I am going to beat the bloody magpie!" He did and our luck changed.

The animals we originally bought were a mixed gathering. They were shorthorns, Friesian crosses, even Herefords. Reggie bought the lot for his suckler herd in Tipperary, allowing us to go to Friesian auctions wherever they might be. We bought what we could, but tried to look into the background of our

stock rather than at the animals themselves. We bought foun-
dation pedigree Friesians, animals whose descendants would
make our name in the future. We bought some duds also. We
said goodbye to the Hereford bull we had inherited from the
previous owners and replaced him with Moneymore Victory,
a bull who did a good job. We got to know the top people in
the breed, people such as Seamus Kelly, John Codd, Michael
Fitzpatrick and many more. They were all dedicated breeders,
men of great ability. By the end of our third or fourth year, our
cows were all black and white, if not all pedigree. Breeders of
Friesians are people of a special nature. The core of these dedicated people is based upon their love of what they do. Their life
is hard, but the best of them can look back at what their parents
did, thus finding justification in encouraging their own children
to follow in their footsteps. These were the people from whom
Gábor and I received advice, friendship and, of course, Pedigree
Friesians.

Within the Friesian breed it is generally accepted, although not
a rule, that one should name every female calf with its mother's
name and a sequential number. Naturally the prefix of the
farmer should precede this. Our prefix became "Robertstown"
so all our animals bore that name first of all, then the name of
the dam, and finally the number she was in the female family. Our cows eventually came to have the name of being reli-
ably bred. This meant that they would perform exactly as
we said they would. Tillystown Molly Bawn 2nd was the first
pedigree animal we bought. All the Mollys that we bred were
descended from her. Over the years the Mollys went all over
the country, sold at our yearly sales. Recently I saw a Molly at
a sale – it did not take long to find out that she was a descend-
ant of Robertstown Molly 22nd. Michael Fitzpatrick bred our
original Molly. He was a well known breeder in his time but
was about to stop milking when we acquired Molly. Although
not one of our best she was a good "middle of the road" cow. I
remember seeing in the north a herd owned by Trevor Gibney.
They were so alike one to the other that it was nearly impossible

for a visitor to differentiate between them. He had obviously used one bull at a time on all the cows over quite a period. I mean he would not have used a variety of bulls to cover animals according to each one's betterment. This is a man who had achieved his own perfection. Gábor never aspired to such an end. He treated each cow individually when deciding on which bull to use. I preferred his approach; it gave more character to the cows.

Herding was an essential part of dairy farming. Every animal had to be inspected daily. Naturally the cows were seen twice a day during milking, but there were at least two groups of heifers as well in different paddocks. First of all one had to see them as a herd, seeing if any of them had separated from the rest. Then whoever was doing the job would count them and afterwards look for signs of mastitis eye disease or any unusual behaviour. If they were "bulling", they were brought in to be served, either by natural service or by A.I. (artificial insemination).

Apart from the fact that Gábor grew up on a farm and had the breeding of animals in his blood, he had worked in Goff's, the famous horse auctioneers, for several years before going to Peru. There he was employed in the tracing of pedigree section. This had to be meticulously done, and he expected the same perfection from his partner in crime, me! I did all the books, registrations, accounts, catalogues, as well as the milking and herding!. The only job I did not do was tractor driving. Working together was good because we were able to discuss all that needed to be done. One of us had to take the responsibility of final decisions and this I left to him. We also milked the animals ourselves during our first ten years. Gábor found a social life extremely difficult during those first years. Cynically he thought that people only invited him as a curiosity, i.e. an Hungarian Baron in Ireland, and thereby he had a justification for his inability to rouse himself from his exhaustion. For my sake he would go, and find himself relaxing into enjoyment after a while.

One of our greatest difficulties was when, once a year, we had to make up our minds on which animals to sell and which to keep. We had our sales at the end of October. It was a time when in September catalogues had to be made and posted shortly before the sale, keeping enough for those who would come to bid on the day. A few days before the sale the cows and heifers had to be washed. This entailed hosing them down and keeping them clean in a separate shed, bedded with straw so thick that we would not have to clean them out. Milking carried on in the background. No matter what happened the milking carried on!

I remember on the occasion of one sale when my niece Sarah, aged about twelve, wished to help. She took upon herself the brushing of the tails, prompting one of those present to remark that if the animals were that quiet he would buy one of them! Years later she regretted not having received a commission!

Calving was a traumatic time. Good records meant that each animal's due date was calculated, and she was watched carefully for signs of parturition as her time approached. Most animals seemed to calve in the middle of the night, giving us time to concentrate on the cow in question. Long hours of sleep were abandoned as we heaved and pulled another calf into this world. Colostrum had to be administered to a shivering calf in the form of beastings (the first milk of a calved cow). In case the cow was unable or unwilling to allow the calf to suck we had to hand feed the calf with stored colostrum. This had to be defrosted very carefully. If one was too hasty and heated the milk too quickly it would become like custard – impossible to administer. I could have willingly given up our enterprise at these moments, longing for my bed and a full night's sleep! Despite the hardship that sometimes found me in tears of tiredness we managed to remain dedicated to the job we had taken on. Gábor sometimes despaired as yet another problem presented itself. Building was a nightmare. Every year we built a new shed to house the expanding herd numbers. These sheds took any excess money we had made, making impossible any idea of enjoyment, apart from inviting and going to friends. Holidays were for other people! We lived for the future. We were supported by the bank. In those days one could trust those who were employed by this institution. They were tough on us, insisted on repayments but we trusted them.

Shortly after we arrived in 1962, the fat-legged Cuban, Scopetta phoned. He was offering Gábor a job. He wanted him to open up a million acres in the Brazilian jungle. It sounded really tempting to me slushing my way in the pouring rain, mud and shit everywhere. Gábor would not budge. As things turned out it was just as well. Climate change and other environmental issues have made such enterprises very suspect.

In about 1965 we began to show our animals, or rather our bulls, at the Bull Show and Sale in the RDS. This Show was only for showing bulls – held in February, it would have been impossible to show cows at this time. It was in two parts. First of all the animals were judged on their confirmation and secondly an auction sold them. At first we did not win any prizes, but we sold our bulls at the subsequent sales. All this happened in the grounds of the Royal Dublin Society. This Society has always been involved in agriculture, and gave us breeders the forum in which to show our produce. We were very conscious of our health status on the farm and never exhibited in any show where the highest standards were not in place. At the time brucellosis and tuberculosis were rife in the country. They are diseases that can ruin a herd. Brucellosis causes infertility and abortion whilst tuberculosis can cause death, in fact will bring about death. We did not wait for the subsidised elimination of these diseases, but at our own cost, with the help of our veterinarian, we became one of the first herds in Ireland to become Brucellosis free.

One of the most important people to us in our first years and afterwards on the farm was our veterinarian, Michael Roe from Naas. He never rushed when examining a cow and never ceased acquainting us with observation and curative techniques. We often had a drink with him after a difficult calving late at night. He had a love for the animals that he looked after, something very special in today's world of mechanisation and endless rhetoric. After Michael's death his assistant, Kevin Dooly took over and did a similar job.

Spring Show at the Royal Dublin Society

Out on grass at home

23

There was little improvement in our style of living in the first few years, but there were compensations. No water and no electricity were beginning to get irksome. We were determined to do something about it soon. I had a great friend, Cicely d'Arcy Irvine, who lived on a farm nearby with her husband, Henry. She invited me to have a bath whenever I wished. Cicely and I used to sit around the fire and talk about her experiences in Burma before the war. They had had to leave their rubber plantation there when the Japanese invaded. Their escape was accomplished with more dignity than many of their colleagues. They left the country by boat and made their way to Kenya. Having stayed there for some months, they returned to Ireland. Henry by then was in his late sixties or early seventies.

Kildare was their choice when they returned here, although they came from Enniskillen. Henry was a great cricketer and enjoyed his game at a club nearby. They were people who had lived life to the full, and were old enough to have experienced a poverty which forced her family to live in Germany when she was a child – she had been born c1890. Her family were unable to run their farm, burdened as they were by the difficulty of providing wages for their employees, to say nothing about supporting the family. People still wandered the roads, and came begging to big houses – it was a sorry time of great suffering. She emigrated with her family and spent several years abroad, in Germany. This was a solution for many of the land-owning families at the time. They would have been what was called Anglo-Irish.

Looking back it is true that there were many beggars populating the roads of Ireland even in the 1940s. They were coated in dirt and lived on the handouts they received. Some very virtuous people kept a loft as a place for them to sleep. Cicely brought all these things alive for me. The stories she had to tell of her varied life were fascinating. When she was in Germany they did not mix with the Germans. Her parents preserved their English/Irish heritage tenaciously, preferring to import English tutors for their offspring than to send them to school in a foreign country. In those days it was deemed unnecessary to educate girls in any way beyond Reading and Writing and Etiquette. The latter was the most important, giving one the necessary distinction of class.

Life was to give her all the education that she needed. She told me of life in Burma. I remember particularly a story she told of the birth, on their farm, of a little boy who would become a well- known politician in London. His mother was Burmese and was servant to their manager who fathered the child. Huge rain made it impossible for the midwife to come and supervise the event, consequently Cicely was the one to deliver the baby. The fact that I had had a similar experience in Peru, without the actual birthing, was a strange sharing that brought with it a bond. Unfortunately, she had glaucoma and had very poor sight when I met her. Little by little she lost her sight altogether. She loved her garden and at first even grew all her vegetables and fruit. A pot at the front door always had some flowers that she would dig up and transfer as needed. Even when totally blind those flowers appeared on the doorstep. She became a person of great importance in my life. I lost her when her daughter decided to sell the house and move to Wexford. There she remained in a strange house with a commode in one room. When it became impossible for her daughter to look after her she was moved into a nursing home in Wexford. There she had a bottle of whiskey with which she had a small cocktail party every night, living out her remaining days with aplomb!

I grew very close to my sister Ita also and enjoyed her children as they came along. Ita would turn up with news of Dublin and of our friends and relations. Occasionally she had a new recipe that I had to taste, she brightened our days, and the children, Graham and Sarah, were enchanting. James and Ita often came to supper, and we returned their visits. There was a certain rivalry, easily resolved, to have Dad come and stay. We always celebrated his arrival in style. He was a man who expected special treatment!

My younger sisters, Elizabeth and Augusta were frequent visitors in the late 1960s. Twins, they were in constant competition with one another. This was all very tongue in cheek, but it amused us enormously. Conor came too, often with his friend Gaby Hogan. They were all full of the joys of life and their youth. Gaby and Conor came here so often that Gábor nicknamed them Beanie and Barney. Beanie and Barny were a well known cartoon couple advertising Baked Beans on television. Our evenings together, with some other friends, often finished with dancing well into the night. The twins were given a car between them, and that little car left its tracks forever on the road between Dublin and Cork. They were given a shop in Cork, a shop that became a boutique called "Les Jumelles", aptly translated by witty Corkmen as "Jumbles". Unfortunately, it never made money as the twins themselves turned out to be the main customers!

Patrick Mansfield was another visitor. Patrick had a large place that he ran with precision. A dear friend, he also came from one of the most persevering landed families in County Kildare. He gave a job to my friend, Doreen Morehead, when she decided to come home to Ireland, having spent some twenty years in London. She lived in our house for about a year, whilst she worked with Patrick. It was fun to have her. She could not get over his insistence that she should start the job by counting sheep. I don't think that she ever managed to get it right, whereas he took great pleasure in teasing her! But she got what she wanted – a job. Later she became curator of Castletown, and, after that, a prime mover in the Wexford Opera festival. She had a great affection for Patrick and often recalled her days as a quasi-farmer. Recently his son Alexander came to lunch with his wife. This was a justification, once again, of our moving to Ireland. Living in the same place for so long brings a sense of continuity which is gratifying. Within the radius of a limited area, in our case, probably twenty miles we knew, or heard of, all the landowners in the county of Kildare. Living in the country has enormous compensations for the lack of city life with its ease of finding entertainment. Tea and dinner parties, cattle shows and trips abroad became our way of life. My parents in Cork always had an open door. They came to stay with us also. They had bought a new house in Passage West in Cork. It is enchantingly beautiful, overlooking the harbour and the river.

Friends from Peru came to inspect us and see what we were doing. Many more came from England. Our Dublin friends came to visit. We had no lack of human contact.

24

One of the main reasons for Gábor's return to Ireland was to initiate more contact with his family and mine. When it became possible to meet his father in the autumn of 1962 he was ecstatic. Because of our contacts in Peru with the British Embassy my father-in-law was allowed to leave Hungary for a short period, with permission to go to Austria. A time limit had been set by the Russians and eighteen years of separation was about to come to an end. Marianne Coreth made her house available to us, and the great day arrived when father and son were reunited. We had fun during those days. He was in the best of form and spoke without stop to his son. To see such joy was to obliterate for a short time all the suffering that they had endured.

Gábor ached for his home. He never spoke about his need and never encouraged others to speak about his pain. Occasionally he would find someone in whom he felt that he could confide, but he always regretted his "weakness" in letting down his guard. Asked if he would return to his farm in northeastern Hungary, he sometimes prevaricated but more often he would go down a tangent of the difficulties of reestablishment. His reply would explain that his home place was far from the markets, that such an enterprise would need the energy of a much younger man, and what would Rosa do in a foreign country with an impossible language! When it did become a possibility he made no effort to return to Hungary – on the contrary, he put the house in the name of the local County Council.

It was thanks to our friend Tom Sewell of the British Foreign Service that we were able to obtain visas to go to Budapest on the death of Gábor's father. Gyorgy had had a heart attack two weeks earlier. Unfortunately as he prepared to go home he suffered a second attack and died.

I met several members of his family, and some of the many friends that he had had, especially Miki Turansky who took us into the countryside and introduced us to some of the loveliest places in Hungary, Esztergom, Visegrád, and Eger. Visegrad is for me one of the most historically interesting places. Even World War 11 is represented in this King Matthias palace. Ruined by generations of invasions it had been completely covered up until it was bombed by the Allies. Uncovered, it displayed wonderful red marble structures, hinting at many more under the rubble. I am told that much more has been revealed in the years since we saw it, in 1963. It is my intention to see it again some day.

In 1962/63 Hungary was still very poor and suffered greatly at the hands of her occupier – Communist Russia. Everywhere we went, be it on trains or busses, there were soldiers, armed and aggressive, treating one and all with contempt. The Rising of 1956 had left its mark. No one could escape the retribution of the common soldier. It was a time of darkness and terror. An enveloping mist covered the city for our first few days and snow made walking difficult. The weather, the white scared faces, the soldiers; all combined to make me realise the hardship that Hungarians had suffered, not only in the war but for the ensuing years after it. Behind closed doors they spoke to Gábor about their plight. We buried his father in Gödöllö, north of Budapest. The snow was deep, and the coffin was open. I stood next to my sister-in-law, Madi, who whispered to me that he was a bad man. It seemed that his treatment of her, after her marriage to Zsigi, had been abominable. He disapproved of the match. He made a mistake. That marriage survived dreadful conditions and suffering. It seems that Hungarians were born to suffer and to condemn one another for being inadequate in the breeding of the next generation! Maybe this was only a trait of the gentry. Certainly he did not approve of our marriage either; in fact I would never have married Gábor if the war had not happened. I was the first foreigner to take the name of Kende in 1,000 years! Now here we all were together

I thought of all that this family had suffered and felt honoured to be there.

With Miki Turanski we travelled for a few days to different parts of Hungary. We first visited Eger. Eger is a massive defensive structure, with underground tunnels containing thousands of gallons of wine. We saw huge containers, and tasted their contents. When the Turks invaded this part of Hungary it was the local women who repulsed them. They manned the fortress and took on the advancing troops with whatever weapons they had to hand.

Esztergom was the main seat of the Hungarian Kings. Here we saw a magnificent Basilica, and wandered through the cobbled streets. I remember the horses, all pulling carts yet with the bearing of carriage horses. They had noble heads with strong necks. They were animals of breeding, animals that had been bred to go to battle when called upon. Just as the men that handled these horses had all the mien of cavalry soldiers, so too had the horses a look of pride.

We spent some time with the family, in this case cousins who had remained in Budapest. We went to the Vár the Buda part of Budapest to find their house. Gábor remembered it well. He had been living there during his university years and the Siege of Budapest. The cousins had a quite large apartment, full of dark corridors and hidden corners. It was a beautiful night, and we stood on a pillared balcony, admiring the city below us and the stars above. There we met Gábor's cousin Helen, and her young niece and nephew. They were the Szentpáli's, and the Szemere's were there too. The object of our get together was to sort out and distribute amongst ourselves precious pieces that had been rescued from Cégény years before by Gábor and his father. The three Kendes were modest to such an extreme that they had to badger one another into accepting anything. Zsigi and Madi were the most reluctant to acquire any possessions. I took it upon myself to bid, ostensibly for us but in fact for them, and made a nice little treasure for them when they finally left Hungary and Roumania.

....

It was Éva, Gábor's sister, who became involved in preserving the family name and in making commemorative photo albums for the next generation. She spoke of the letters in Cégény and of how they were a family treasure. It had been a great tragedy for all when one half disappeared. In 1979 Éva wrote to her two brothers asking them if they would agree to allow her to hand over their half of the letters to the Hungarian government which was, at that time, still under Russian communist rule. Her fear was that, unless something was done, the letters would end up in a wastepaper basket, dumped by future generations who would not recognise their value. The communists had been responsible for throwing the Kendes out of their home in 1945. It was not only our family who lost everything but also anyone who had any possession, estate or small holding. It was a brave decision of Éva's, one that was not approved of by many of the noble classes. She was always brave and refused to allow history to be revised by men of small minds. She saw that the letters between Kölcsey and Kende (another Zsigmond) merited a place in one of the museums in Budapest. Both Zsigi and Gábor agreed with her, and she wrote to the Minister of Culture.

The Hungarian government responded with alacrity, and in 1980 Ernö Taxner, a museum director, travelled to Switzerland to meet her and to find out what we wanted in return. The three Kendes, Gábor, Zsigi and Éva Pestallozzi, were unanimous in that they did not want money, but suggested that a reunion of the family in Hungary might be a good idea. The Hungarians agreed. Our family also asked for a permanent exhibition of the letters to be mounted in Budapest. We asked for the preservation of the family crypt in Cégény. There was a fear that it would be flooded by the removal of a dyke between the Park in front of the house and the river Szamos. We also asked that the monument to the war dead in the village should include the names of Baron Gyorgy, who served in the First World War, and Gyorgy junior, who was killed in the Second. Another item was the preservation of the mill in Istvándi. They agreed. They did everything and arranged a wonderful two weeks for us, with Daisy, Éva and Richard. Madi and Zsigi travelled all the way from Canada. The government had a special block of apartments for guests. There we were in luxury, with Madi and Zsigi in the next apartment. Imagine our surprise when Taxner told us that they had already in their possession the other half of the letters! How they got them, or when, or where, we have no idea. I have a feeling that if Éva had not offered them our side of the letters, all the letters might have ended up in that proverbial waste paper basket! Instead they are on permanent exhibition in the Irodalmi Museum in Budapest. The Museum Directors invited a goodly number of our friends and theirs to a splendid opening ceremony in September 1981. The Museum is an imposing building with a lovely stairway leading from the hall to the first floor where the letters were beautifully mounted in glass cases. A large painting of Kölscey contributed to the imposing effect. Éva was overcome to see the result of her generosity. The Minister spoke about the letters and congratulated the family for its gift, he also spoke about the letter's historical importance, and of how welcome their return to Hungary was. He hoped that we would enjoy our stay in Budapest and announced that he would join us in Cégény.

Next day we set out for Cégény   It had been a long journey from Budapest, some six hours driving, and we were tired when we reached Mátészalka. Four poster beds and a huge delight of satin bedspreads and cushions all glimmering in red, furnished our bedroom for the next seven days. Somehow I did not expect to drive through so many little villages with their flower bedecked houses. Unlike Ireland, none of the houses faced the road – they were sideways on. Mátészalka is famous for being the birth place for a very well known American film star – Tony

Curtis. It is also infamous, infamous for the massacre of its large Jewish population during World War 11.

We had two interesting visits in the town. The first was to meet the Agricultural Museum Director, József Farkas. Old farm machinery and implements fascinated both Gábor and Zsigi. Memories abounded as they exclaimed over carts and hay forks, the likes of which they had not seen in many years. József was also a writer. He wrote of the people of Mátészalka and its surrounding districts. Among his books was one in English translation that was written about the Kendes, and how they were in the twelfth or thirteenth century. He wrote of a territorial family, who fought for their land and their women, measuring everything by these two main principles. All was subservient to this, witnessed by the fact that they embraced or relinquished their Catholicism as fancy took them. They were wild, arrogant and always ready to fight to preserve what was theirs. He gave me his book, but I made the mistake of reading bits of it to Gábor. When I looked for it recently, it had gone. There is no doubt that Gábor spirited it away, not liking to admit to the intransigence of his ancestors! Our second visit was to meet an old friend of Zsigi's with his wife. Although small the house was carefully furnished with a few pieces of lovely furniture and one or two nice pictures that proclaimed their owner's past. He had been the owner of a neighbouring estate and a great friend of all the family.

Then it was time to go to Cégény. About half an hour from Mátészalka we turned off the main road. By now it was twilight. Gábor told me where to put the car, and we walked towards the house. It was dramatic. It was the first time that he had seen it since he had to leave in 1945. In 1981 the three of us, Gábor, me and Daisy, holding hands, stood together. The house reflected the sinking sun, its yellow turning to a burnished gold. Somehow it welcomed us back, as memories of their lives here brought tears to the eyes of Gábor, Éva, and Zsigi. It was a moment that none of us will forget.

Kölcsey was asked to write a dedication to the house on a plaque when it was first built. It was translated for me by Tamas Kabdebo, the well known author.

Working hands created me on

The bank of the blond Szamos

The poet saw me there and sent his message to me.

"House, you are!

Keep your Master, his children, grandchildren in your lap

Letting them inherit you with joy.

Such evocative words and the care that the children had been unable to provide rankled. Recently I heard Communism being described as a concept out of fashion and totally destructive in its inception. Such cryptic aphorisms reflect the agony and disruption of millions, cast out of their homes to wander the earth for the rest of their days. Those who stayed in Hungary did so in the knowledge that their lot would be poverty and possible starvation. Gábor's father dedicated his life in Budapest to making a genealogical work, charting in great detail the progeny of the four heroes celebrated in Hero Square. People in his village in the country sent him eggs, apples and flour with other produce from their little plots. Also from the village, a woman called Erzsi looked after his washing and cleaning. Gábor and Éva sent him money through the Red Cross. This arrived as food parcels that he then converted into cash. It became a bearable life for him amongst the Communists. He wrote of daily trips to the Baths. These are a feature of Budapest, famous worldwide. They are relaxing and exercise the body without huge effort. He had relations and friends also whom he enjoyed visiting. Most of his time, however, was spent in the Archives looking for the necessary information for his work.

He lived in a tiny room, crammed full with a bed, a desk, and boxes of items he had managed to retrieve before the Russian arrival. Because of his lack of space, he found a friend who was willing to house his files until he finished. Gábor and I saw those files in that house and found it hard to credit that his father had physically done so much. There were no computers in those days.

We were greeted by the Director of the orphanage. The house accomodated 100 gypsy children. We met them all. Evidently they were very disappointed to meet us as we were dressed in jeans. They expected us to arrive with crowns on our heads! Their teachers had prepared them for our arrival with stories of royalty!

Next day there were great celebrations to honour the return of the letters. In the great hall of Cégény there was a reception for us, a few selected villagers and some of the older orphans. We were welcomed by the Minister, carefully monitored by television cameras. After a few more speeches, it was Zsigi's turn to speak. He had definitely come home, and he spoke with emotion and huge dignity. From being the joker of the family, he came into his own as the head of it. Then the books were produced. The government had published all the letters in one volume, copies of which were to be distributed to all present. After this surprise, we Kendes had to sign dozens of copies, each one of us, even little Daisy!

We were called into lunch. There were more speeches and plenty to eat and drink. The staple food in the country is boiled meat with vegetables. This is usually preceded by the soup made in the process of cooking the meat for the main course. Afterwards there were lots of heavy puddings. Daisy and I were delighted to be sitting in what used to be the drawing room of her grandfather's house. Hungarian was spoken all around us as we indulged in speculation as to how things had been before. The house, now an orphanage, had no pictures, nor any of the accoutrements of a family home. Yet there was plenty to imagine as we peopled our surroundings with children of Daisy's age, now nine, and parents, the mother in a wheelchair and the other, a proud and worried Gyorgy.

More ceremony followed in Istvandi at the Mill. This is a flour mill, erected in the thirteenth century, of unique beauty, in a wonderful setting. A complicated system of waterways creates a lake and a race to work the mill wheel. Surrounding all this, there are woods and fields with a bridge leading to a pathway to what used to be a house – the home of Zsigmond and Ilona. Unfortunately the house no longer exists. The little that remains has been turned into a school. Nowadays the place is full of tourists, swimming in the lake, picnicking and camping. Whole schools come for a week at a time. Their busses are neatly parked, nearly out of sight. The Mill is in working order, and can operate on special occasions.

Our ceremony in 1981 was a special occasion, and the old mill hand was there. He was beaming as he greeted Gábor, Éva and Zsigi. For the first time since after the war, his mill was working, and he was in his element again! My father-in-law should have been there. His adjustment to a new order in Budapest, staying in his beloved country, dedicating himself to his studies showed an understanding of human nature that forgave the invaders for his debasement. He would have understood what his family had done. They had returned priceless papers to mark the history of their country, a gesture that ignored politics and indicated an awareness of future historians delving into their country's past.

Many of Gábor's school friends had heard that we were in Budapest, and consequently we were invited to their homes. The Turanskys lived in an apartment of only three rooms on the top floor overlooking the Danube and the Chain bridge, in a house that used to belong to them, in days before the advent of the Russians. Miki was a great friend of Gábor's at school, and later. Gábor gave him a Kende silver cup. This cup carried the name of the man with the best bag (of game) after the shoots in Cégény. Miklós was still a great shot and fisherman. Unfortunately, he died before we went to Budapest again, but his sons either use the cup or sold it. Gábor did not care which. He felt that the cup was the least he could do for the family. Their daughter, in later years came to stay with us in Ireland.

We spent another evening with the Hatvanyi family. It was there that I became aware of the role of the grandmother in Hungarian families. Everyone worked, albeit for very little money, and yet they continued to make children. Having had her children, the mother returned to work, leaving the grand-mother at home to look after the little ones. The effect at that time of this change in family roles could be seen on the streets leaving them completely empty during the day, followed by overcrowding when work stopped. It was strange for us to see such lack of coordination. In the Hatvanyi household there was a little girl of Daisy's age who directed all her little queries to her grandmother. I felt sorry for the mother. Although mothers have paid jobs nowadays in this country, I have not noticed that the streets have become empty during the day. But I have noticed that between 6 p.m. and later the food shops have become full of bustling young women, always in a hurry.

Years later, in about 1983, Éva was told about the Russians' arrival in Cégény. Standing on the steps of the entrance, a Russian officer summoned the villagers and told them to help themselves to the furniture, the silver and the paintings in the house. They did not delay! The parson's wife came rushing up crying, "May I too have something of the Baron's wealth?" "But of course," came the reply. Taking care, she helped herself to two large pictures. She it was who kept for us those two pictures in her own house, until one day, nearly forty years later, spotting Éva in the village, she invited her in and told her the story. One of these pictures hangs today in our house in Ireland, the other is with Gábor's nephew, another Gábor, in Canada. The picture we have is by Ferenczy Valér, son of the famous Ferenczy. It is called "The Three Graces"   This picture was a wedding present to Gábor's parents in 1914.   It was painted in 1908 by a man who reputedly only painted two other pictures in his life.   His father, who painted in a more traditional fashion was deeply ashamed of his son's work.   It was a big present given to Gábor's parents at a cost of 1,400 sovereigns.   Their neighbours and friends got together to pay for it and to make the presentation.   It remains our pride and joy.   We have to thank Éva for retrieving it.   Having found the picture, she went about trying to acquire it legally according to the Communist rule. She discovered that we could buy it!!!!!!!!!!   This was quite risible to Gábor, but he remembered the picture and parted with the £350 that secured our ownership.   I think that this money secured the purchase of the other picture as well.

Amongst the many relations and friends that we met in Budapest was Margó, a cousin of Gábor's.   Later, when we revisited Hungary, her second husband, Edé, became a very important friend and mentor for Gábor.   They had a great mutual respect and love for one another, and it was wonderful for them both to be together once a year.   Edé was the only person that I knew in Gábor's life who fulfilled a father role for Gábor.   He had friends, yes, but this was special.   Edé is a lawyer and a man of great humanity.   Margó was his most devoted wife and substitute mother to his daughters.   His first wife had died several years previously.   Later we helped him in having two of his grandchildren come under our guardianship to school in Ireland.   This was when we first noticed the large gap that had evolved between Eastern and western Europe during the forty years of the Russian occupation of the East.   The gap was cultural.   The years of occupation and all that it entailed meant that two generations of Hungarians had lived under the tensions created by an alien and intrusive government. They are a proud people, a people steeped in their history. They lived in a state of terrified rebellion and compromise.   Unless one joined the Communist Party there was very little possibility of a full education.   These were people who had led the world in the fields of the Sciences and Mathematics.

Their occupiers were a race of incredibly obtuse men. They were indeed men who were not of the land, but of politics inspired by jealousy and hatred.

....

It was about twenty years after her father's death, some time in the '90's that Éva decided it was her duty to remove the two Gyorgy who had been buried in Gödöllö and to reinter them in the family crypt in Cégény. This was the most difficult undertaking that she had ever tackled. The paper work was horrendous but she prevailed, and, with the two coffins, she made the trip by train all the way to Cégény and the park. To take the bones of a beloved father and brother to their predestined resting place was both emotionally and physically exhausting. This is the stuff of which she was made. She could not turn back the pages of history, but she fulfilled a very important end to their lives.

Gábor with his father

A shared joke

25

Some time in the 1960's Pat and John Baugh sent their son Lionel from Peru to school in Ireland. They had been very good friends of ours in South America and were anxious that their sons should have an Irish education. We offered to look after the boys. Lionel went to Headfort, a boarding school in Kells, Co. Meath. His free weekends and holidays were spent with us. Because of him we met the Hickson family, or rather I met Daphne at a party in Dublin, and learnt that she had two sons of the same age as Lionel. The following year Lionel's brother Charles Baugh arrived also. The four boys became firm friends. John bought a canoe for Lionel, and the boys made full use of it, even going on the canal down to the River Shannon. Tim Mansfield joined this little gang in their dare-devil pursuits. Tim was Brownie's son. She was married to her second husband, Johnny Mansfield.

Patrick Mansfield married Elizabeth and they had three children, Alexander, Louisa, and James. I always thought that Elizabeth introduced high class cooking to Kildare. She was to lift the standard right through the county. She also introduced us to many new friends and was a great party mum for the children. The Mansfields lived in a great dark house, full of creaking rooms and stairs. It was all very romantic. I remember an evening when we all went swimming in the River Liffey full of good food and wine. It was dark and the water was cold, but it was great. It sobered us. Hair wet, in our underclothes, we used up every towel in the house. Ita was there too that night, but not James. Gábor did not join us in the river, but enjoyed watching.

The daily routine of milking carried on. Up at six o'clock in the morning Gábor or I struggled down and managed to have the churns out at 8 a.m. in time for the lorry that came from Dublin every day. During the first year or two, before electricity, starting the diesel pump was a difficulty. Sometimes it would take half and hour to get going. Gábor would get more and more frustrated and angry as the "fucking thing" wouldn't start. The cows would sense his mood and the milk production would suffer. I never attempted to start the milking machine and, consequently, became the "better" milker until we installed electricity.

In those days, to get electricity and a telephone in this benighted country of ours, one had to have "pull". "Pull" meant that an application for these services was absolutely useless unless you had the support in writing of the local TD. The appointed recipient of the application would invariably explain that there might be a delay of a couple of years, whereupon Gábor would get in touch with anyone that he knew of influence. Nothing stopped him hammering on doors as he ignored excuses and letters indicating how difficult our area was and how many people were ahead of us in the queue. One of the reasons given for many refusals was the fact that electricity had been turned down when offered some years back by the inhabitants of our road, who feared that their houses might be set on fire by the demon electricity!

When we finally got our telephone, we were beleaguered by the operator with whom we had to get in touch before making a call. She had a rota of her own of "putting us through". Always listening to calls, I presume she found us boring since so many calls of ours were in languages she did not understand. Country post offices tend to breed their own inquisitive and sometimes even destructive types. Used to the anonymity of city telephones, it was a great relief when the phone became automatic. The antideluvian state we had bought into was finally brought up to modern standards with electricity, water and communication by 'phone some two years after we took up residence.

Our road of Newtown Donore was a very rural place in those days. There were people here that had never been to Dublin. Naas (8 kilometers away) was an expedition that might be planned for days. The clip-clop of horse-drawn carts was the only sound from the road. If a car passed, it was an occasion. Despite this, or maybe because of this, we were able to draw our help from the houses around. Boys like Dan Ward and Feg Pender made good helpers. At silage and hay making their fathers and others came to help. A difficult calving also necessitated neighbourly help. Day or night, they would arrive, ready to assist at the birth of another Robertstown calf. Each and everyone of us would feel gratification if all went well, or if not, then whisky would be called on for consolation. If it were at night, we would not return to bed until the calf had had its beastings (in human terms – colostrum).

I spoke of whisky but tea, in fact, was the order of the day. Harvest teas, if the weather was good, were often partaken in the field where hay was made. Neighbours arrived to help. We would sit comfortably on the hay and eat sandwiches of ham or egg, cakes and biscuits. Milk fresh from the cow was often the preferred drink of our guests. The sun shone and the men were hot. Gábor worked with them, pouring sweat, as he forked hay into cocks. They had good fun together, rather dulled by my presence until I gathered up the things and drove back to the house.

It was my turn to milk with Dan one morning when, looking out at the yard from my bedroom, I saw Dan lying flat on the milk trolley. He had been complaining of a back pain for a few days, but back pain was one of the hazards of the job. We were not too worried. However, seeing him like that I knew that he needed assistance. He was taken to Naas Hospital. After a few days they told him to go home. They told me that he had been malingering. To me that was ridiculous. I had seen the distress he had been in. Having got used to the system in my country of "it is not what you know, but whom you know", I rang a friend who had an important position in St. James' hospital in Dublin. He immediately arranged for Dan to go to St. James's. They found a tumour, operated and, wonderfully, discovered it to be benign. Donald Weir told me afterwards that Dan's tumour was written up in medical journals as being an extraordinary case.

All this time we were buying more cows and grading up (to pedigree) others. Gradually we came to the point where we had to take the Friesian Society as more than just a place to register our animals. The registering was done on cards, and each calf had to be drawn on its card, its markings blacked in exactly. The sire and dam were noted down with their pedigree numbers. The system worked well. This identification process was essential to showing and selling. All milk was recorded weekly, showing exactly how much each animal produced and a supervisor came to check our figures on a regular basis. We also kept a diary of everything that happened on the farm.

Gábor had a real talent for breeding. He managed over the years that we were farming to take the modest animals that we had bought into being amongst the best in the country. This he did without spending a lot of money, although we did import some good animals from England. He appreciated a cow's faults as much as her good points, and always tried to improve everything a little in the next generation. Longevity rated high on his list – he was not impressed by exhaustingly high milk yields. A cow that never takes a rest will die early.

Each year the money that we earned was more than the year before. Our firm belief was that we had to take care of the cows, and put them first. We did not have to sacrifice ourselves too much – there was always enough to eat and drink, and during the 1960s Nancy looked after us and the house. Lionel and Charles brightened up our lives in no uncertain fashion. Lionel was keen to do everything on the farm, and I can still see him carrying a bale of hay on his head, proving his ability to carry it. We had a pony for him, but we were both too busy to teach him how to ride. It was a pity, but he found other amusements. Sometimes the boys got into terrific fights, and Nancy would come shouting for me, "Lionel is killing Charles". They survived. Anna and Peter Simpson also took an interest in the boys. Because their first education had been in Peru, their knowledge of Irish and English history was pretty poor, and Peter became their coach in these subjects. Their capabilities improved, and soon they were coping quite well in school.

Charles, Lionel and Sheila Baugh

26

It was in 1973 that Ireland joined the European Common market. Endless discussion and anticipation preceded this giant step for Ireland into the global world. Everyone waited to see what would happen next, but my dear husband was convinced that his salvation had arrived. He was back in Europe!

Until 1969 we used a bucket plant for milking. This involved the use of at least two people milking and the lifting and carrying of buckets to the coolant system. Shaped like a washboard, the cooler was served by running water from the well. The milk had to be lifted above shoulder height into a container which in turn fed it in such a way that it trickled over the cold pipes of the cooler underneath, and from there to a churn. A cow might give five gallons at a time. It was hard work. As the milk increased it became obvious that we should install a milking parlour. In a milking parlour we would only have to put on or take off the clusters or cups on the cow's teats. Everything else would be automatic. Gábor decided to get a job so that we would be able to pay for the construction of a new parlour. For three years he drove every weekday to Swords in County Dublin to run a mink farm. He hated the idea of it, but it paid sufficiently well to build our parlour. I ran the farm with an extremely good lad – Eamon Dempsey – whilst Gábor was gone. Eamon was typical of the best in Kildare. Highly intelligent, with a great gift with animals, he reminded us of Peter Mulhern. Coming from a farm himself, he was also wary of spending and a great help.

There is no doubt that Gábor really hated the mink job. The very idea of feeding animals so that they should have good coats was abhorrent. Having to kill them in the end was also abhorrent. Finally he woke one night with a bad pain. Doctors and ambulances brought him to the Mater Hospital where he was found to have a perforated ulcer. Eamon took over the farm as I followed Gábor to Dublin for the night. I stayed with Ita and James. As always they were kindness itself, and Ita came with me to see Gábor next day. He was in good hands. I returned to the farm. Brian Hederman, a friend and physician was in charge of him, and we were assured that Brian was the very best. He looked after Gábor well, so well that he did not need an operation. It was nearly Christmas when he came home, after three weeks in hospital. Ita and James helped me a great deal, and later I was very happy that I had seen so much of her in those days. I went to see Gábor in hospital every day after milking.

.

It was a miserable evening – rain and cold. I was sitting by the fire, waiting for Ita and James to arrive, when the telephone rang. Gábor picked it up and was informed by the police about the accident. I wandered down the house and found him with his hands cradling his head as he sat in the dining room. He was shattered and, on my asking what had happened, he pointed to the phone and said, "Ring the police". I did. He was unable to give me such bad news. I rang the police. I started to wail in a muted fashion, but constantly, through the night, through the next and subsequent days. The family all came. Dad was wonderful – how strong he was, and how brave. His shoulder was necessary. Gábor too was fantastic but he was still very weak. Ita was in a car accident. The children were there too, but escaped. James was driving but escaped unhurt. She had been coming to see Gábor, who was still in a bad shape. She was, after all, a nurse. She was also bringing the Christmas cake.

Ita's death filled the family with sadness and tragedy. In my case, she was not only my sister, but also my best friend. Our friendship had grown out of our sisterhood, but it was unique. We not only knew the best of one another, but the worst too. She was my confidant. She knew of my friendship with Cicely and once hearing that she was sick, offered to come down to wash my bedridden friend. The nurse that she was was always there, she could not stand aside when her help was needed. Such was she – nobody could come to her in need without a response. But on top of that she was fun, fearless and devoted to her two little children. We buried her on Christmas Eve. Even now, all those years later, I cry as I write, I cry because I still miss my little sister.

My sister Ita

27

Since we had returned to Ireland the Pestalozzi family came to see us for several weeks every second summer. They spent alternate summers in Roumania and Hungary thereby widening their childrens' outlook. Éva came on inspection, always keen on the welfare of her siblings. The result for me was that of being in a goldfish bowl, or a puppet dancing to her tune. She was a good woman but she did want everyone to be in her mould. She loved to take charge! Having visited us she would go to inspect Madi and Zsigi in Roumania, and her father in Hungary. The fact that her husband, Richard, was a Swiss diplomat gave them the right to travel behind the Iron Curtain. Madi had an easier time than I – she understood all the languages. Hungarian, German, a little French and English were all spoken during their visits.

When they came to Ireland they would usually make a trip to Connemara, Cork, or Kerry during their stay. Éva was, of course, Gábor's sister. The main topic of conversation was about their brother, Zsigi. Zsigi was stuck in Roumania, in Transylvania, the part that used to be Hungary. The final meeting to discuss the consequences of the Second World War took place in Yalta, under the auspices of Stalin, Churchill, and Roosevelt, the brave men who took upon themselves the carving up of Europe, and, in doing so, stripped Hungary of huge tracts of land. They were three men who had become heroes of the world but who by now were burnt out and old. They decided against all historical facts that Hungary should be stripped of Trannsylvania, thereby punishing her for not backing the Allies in the war. Transylvania was where the Kendes' mother's property lay and where Zsigi was doing his best to eke out a living. Hungarians in that area were harassed, not only by the Russians but also by the Roumanians. On top of that, they deprived one of Zsigi's sons of the completion of his education. Food always had to be queued for, ex-landlords always having to take the last place. If they seemed to be on their way up in a successful business, they were stopped and forced to abandon the enterprise. This is a well-documented story, but one that should not be forgotten. The Kendes suffered mightily but so did everyone else. The Russians were not unique in their cruelty. They manifested their own stupidity only because they knew no better. Communism lost in the end, like Hitler, through Stalin's self importance and the rejection of any experienced politicians available.

Gábor and Éva were determined to remedy Zsigi and Madi's situation. As a family they were devoted to one another, and it was good to see their anxiety to make life better for their brother and his wife. It started on our return from Peru. It took a long time to reach success. It seemed that the best way to go was to use Richard Pestallozzi's contacts. Being in the Swiss diplomatic corps he had good contacts. He tried everything to no avail. Éva did the same. Finally Gábor and I went to see our local TD, Gerard Sweetman who was also a firm friend of my father. Gerard had another friend, Freddie Boland who happened to be President of the United Nations. Thus it was that wheels within wheels, and whom you know, worked, and the entire family were allowed to travel, thanks to Freddie Boland. For the two young men, another Gábor, and Balint, it was exciting to leave Roumania. There, there was no future for them, but for their parents, already in their 60's it was difficult. Even though they had suffered so much over the years, Madi and Zsigi had friends and a way of life that they understood. Zsigi and the boys spoke no English, but Madi did. She was the one who would find it easy to adapt. She found a job, in Castletown, mending Aubusson carpets, and she went to England to do a course in china mending. She was resourceful and ambitious for Zsigi and herself. Gábor, or I should say, young Gábor, found a job in the Avoca mines. Balint helped on the farm. It seemed as though they might prosper.

Young Gábor went to Canada.   He suffered from his back, but managed to get a teaching job in Toronto.   This lasted for a few years, but his back disimproved.   Eventually he had to cease work, and took invalid payment from the government. He married and had four children, but, sadly, his marriage ended in divorce.   In time his interests returned to Hungary. He went to Cégeny, and stayed there for several months at a time.   He rang his Uncle Gábor whenever there seemed to be movement in the attitude of the local hierarchy as regards the Kende house and its lands.   He gave us good advice when the conversion of the compensation we had received for the theft of Cégeny became a possibility of being converted to a pension scheme   The Hungarians paid the pension until my husband's death.   The recompense was a condition laid down by the EU for Communist Hungary when they wanted to join. It came as quite a surprise to us.   We had given up all hope of anything being returned.

Before he died Gábor repeatedly told me to get in touch with the Embassy as soon as he was gone.   His determination to show his countrymen honest and straightforward dealing was linked to a shame that he felt for the new Hungary. He had an idealised notion of the landlords of the past and always represented them. I always suspected that his knowledge of his country was based on the emotional values of a twenty year old boy – the age he was when he escaped.   Known for his own honesty and truthfulness in business, he was admired by one and all within our community.   For instance, if it be-came routine to charge more every year for a bull, his sense of fairness did not allow him to charge inflated prices.   This did not mean that in any way he was a "soft touch".   It was quite the opposite.   He would fight to the utmost to secure a fair deal.   His dealings with the "New" Hungarian government and his pension became a question of noblesse oblige.   I had my directions and I cancelled the pension about a week after his death.   They belied his opinion of them by behaving very generously with me.

Zsigi, Gábor jnr., and Tom Doyle

Balint, Rafi Rupert, Gábor

28

In 1966 a magnificent film, made by RTE (the Irish television station), was shown each week to celebrate the 50th Anniversary of the Easter Rising against the British occupation of Ireland. Brilliantly executed, the several episodes became compulsive viewing for the entire population. It was graphic and amazing. We all knew the story of those heroic men, and as the weeks progressed talk became heated, as many people found new allegiances in the portrayal. It was exciting as the majority renewed their commitment to their Irishness. Gábor was the only person I knew who was not carried away. He found it to be dangerous, tapping on deep-seated prejudices. He had plenty of experience. He had seen the same whipping up of peoples' emotions in his own country. In short he feared the worst, and he was right.

A blow from the Unionists, echoing the stupidity with which they managed their nefarious affairs since 1922 and centuries before, brought a new response. The IRA struck back. As always happens throughout history, the Irish Republican Army became strong through its own initiation. Young men were attracted by the excitement of the adventure. Some were idealistic, but mostly they were young people who only knew poverty and longed to fulfil themselves.

Listening to old soldiers, the descriptions they give of their experiences in the Second World War are given with pride, in fact a pride superseding any other aspects of their lives. They have been to areas where their basic fears and ecstasies have been tested. They have grown to understand cowardice and tears. It is a lucky man who has been there, and if he has, then he will be capable of understanding the frailties of others. Unfortunately, many only see their combat experiences as a static story to be repeated *ad nauseam*. Such men are the stuff of which mens' clubs are made.

In time the soldiers of the IRA will enjoy recounting their exploits – there will be an awful lot to be ashamed of and of which they will not speak, but they will have known what fear is and ecstasy. Away from war, killing and survival, it is possible in sport and adventure to reach the depths and heights of which we are capable. The emotions that can reach dangerous, albeit wonderful extremes include love, hate, sorrow, patriotism, utopianism. These were all attractive means to a solution given by the IRA and their opponent Unionists to many of humdrum existence. Huge injustice has been wrought in our country in the name of religion, to say nothing of the thousands dead.

But they eventually achieved some equality between Catholics and Protestants. Looking at Ian Paisley as leader of the country is just as improbable as having Martin Mc Guinness and Gerry Adams in positions of power. Somehow this is reminiscent of Kenya in the 1950s. The Mao Mao revolution under Kenyatta was tireless in its murder of the white, often English, proprietors of land in the country. After a final success he became president and was introduced to Queen Elizabeth. I am quite certain that our three bandits will receive the same honour. This is the beginning of the end, an end that will finally put a stop to the mayhem of the past 35 years. Many people name this or that leader of government as the main arbiter of peace, but in fact it was the people themselves who finally were able to confess that lasting peace was the only path to take. Long may it last!

29

I had a dream before my sister was killed. We were on the dunes near Rosslare Harbour. We watched an aeroplane flying south, and disappearing. I wonder why our cows were with us and why too they disappeared over the cliffs. I turned around and Ita was no longer with me. Three disappearances. I woke. It was such a vivid dream that I told Gábor all about it. Four hours later we heard that an Irish plane had crashed on its way to Wales, carrying many of the top men in Irish business, some from a factory in Newbridge – Irish Ropes. For days rescuers looked for the crashed plane in the Welsh mountains, and I was sorely tempted to ring and tell them about my dream. I did not, mostly for fear that they would just laugh. Finally the plane was found near the Tusker Rock, in other words <u>south</u> of Wexford, and not where it should have been, in the Welsh mountains. Now in hindsight I truly believe that my dream witnessing the crash was a warning for me about Ita's death.

Ita's and James' two children became part of our lives, as I tried to fulfil a promise I had made to her before her death. Only a month before she died she asked me to look after them. This I did to the best of my ability. Naturally it was their father who was in charge, and he employed good people to look after them. My role was to have them down to the farm as much as possible. They helped me with my grief also. James remarried some three years later.

We decided to celebrate Graham's birthday on the farm, after Ita's death. We provided shelter with piled up straw bales in a cow shed ensuring that the weather would not spoil our plans. The children could eat there, surrounded by balloons and party favours. But we had no need to worry. The afternoon was perfect, and the little ones had a really lovely time. There was plenty of help since all the mothers stayed – most of them came from Dublin.

I remember Graham gathering up all his toys and presents and taking them into a room where he could be alone. There he was able to enjoy them.

In the middle of the party an American friend of ours turned up. He had been sent to us by Joan Gildemeister some years before. We had known Joan in Peru, before she divorced her husband, Enrique. Robert Reese was a speech writer for the Treasurer of the United States and his work brought him to Ireland originally. One of his assignments was to write about antiquities and monuments here. We were the only contact he had. We introduced him to a couple of people in the field and to the Matuschkas, who have a High Cross on their land – the Cross of Moone.

This time he brought a beautiful young girl with him who was called Jeannie Rowlands. Jeannie was coming to Ireland to study Irish history. Robert Reese hoped that we would help look after her. I was delighted to have her stay. It meant that I could speak about all the thoughts and ideas that provoked me to a willing ear! She probably stayed for a few months. It really was lovely having her.

There was a terrible emptiness in my life after Ita's death. Time and again my fingers would start dialling her number, used as they were to doing so on a daily basis. But it was not only me – the entire family was in mourning, and all we could do was remember. Then of course the dreadful killing started in the North. Every day would bring news of numbers, always numbers, - numbers counting the dead. There was no room in the news to speak about court cases in those days. Nowadays we feel the necessity to teach our children about the Holocaust in order to educate them not to emulate such horrors. It seems that they are so innocent that there is a fear that they might become arrogant in self-righteousness. I wonder if we cannot trust them.

It was a difficult time to go through. But now, in 2009, I think that it had a final result that might compensate for the horrors that had to be endured. It has been a festering wound for far too long. The incredible self-delusion of the British in thinking that their might is always right left the Irish in a state of shock, unable to stand behind the IRA, and yet equally unable to criticise the Unionists. It took decades, and the Americans to arrive at some solution. In time the protagonists will become heroes and politicians.

Robert Reece, friend from the States sent by Joan Gildemeister

Charlotte Reece with
Pisco and Mossy

30

In 1972 the most wonderful thing was that our daughter Daisy was born. Her arrival meant, once again, a new beginning in our lives. Friends, family and neighbours all flocked to see the "miracle baby"! She was born in a delightful hospital in Dublin in the days when one's health insurance paid for a lovely room with a balcony in the Mount Carmel Hospital. Augusta, my sister, had looked after everything for me during the last few months of my pregnancy. She and I took Daisy home and had to learn from a neighbour, Joy Weld, how to change a nappy! We were still in the days of cloth nappies, and pins. The modern ones were available but very expensive, and not as absorbent as they are today.

Daisy was a delight. It was strange that I, who had never been interested in tiny people, suddenly found the days too short to express my love for this little person. Her dependence on me was both flattering and rewarding. Breast feeding for two months was difficult but amazing. I empathised with the cows and understood their agony when their calves were taken away. It was such a happy time. When cows are under stress for whatever reason their milk production suffers, just so it was with me when Gábor took me for a walk of inspection down the farm. I had help and was delighted to go but on returning to my baby, found that I was completely dry – no milk! Panic buying of bottles and powdered milk ensued, leaving me feeling both guilty and relieved!

....

Joining the Common Market put paid to any budgeting we may have had. Remuneration went up, but so did costs. The latter introduced a new concept, as our expences rose by some 200%. Used to small margins we had to adjust and above all

192

understand the economics. It turned out to be in our favour. As I have said before, Gábor was highly over-qualified for our little farm. Not only had he run San Jacinto, but he also had been involved with the running of the family place in Hungary. The fact that he had studied Economics at university also contributed enormously to our continuing success, a success not reflected in our bank balance!

From the day we took over, the farm had risen in value year by year. We had a milking parlour with a good collection yard, a slurry pit and sheds to house the ever increasing number of cows. Percentage increase in our capital was of no particular interest, but it was reassuring, just like having an assured capital base in Government Bonds. In our case it was demonstrated in the knowledge that we always had collateral for our business in farming. Daisy came to us at the right time. Her education was never a problem where money was concerned.

Gábor had a deep commitment to the success of the place. His background, where it had been in Hungary, filled him with a desire, akin to that of his father's, to restore the family fortunes. The importing of his family in 1969 was a very big step in that direction. He loved Ireland, he also loved Hungary, but his real commitment was to the Kende family. This was in no way a thing of nepotism, it was more that of an enveloping union with the land of his fathers, and with the people not only of his blood, but also those who had either worked with the Kendes or been friends with them. His loyalty was without question. For years he never spoke about his loss of land – in fact he spoke only of bovine matters, boring hostesses all over the county! Horsy people are identical. They think, talk and dream of nothing else. But Gábor could make us laugh in his seriousness. He was particularly funny when with friends, or the men on the farm. One of them told me recently that when an east wind blew he cryptically christened it as being "From Russia with love". An east wind always did a lot of damage!

A great day came in 1972 (I was enormous with Daisy), when we won the top Friesian Bull prize at the Royal Dublin Society. We not only won the championship that year, but also the Reserve Championship. They made good prices at the subsequent sale and influenced interest in our stock. Our yearly sales of surplus stock did well. We always tried to cover our expenses with our milk income. The yearly sale was the cream.

Because of more confidence in what we were doing, and to a great extent Daisy's birth, we decided to knock down the cottage and, following its lines, built a two-story house in its place. It was arduous but we were still young, and we had Bertha Usquiano from San Jacinto to look after our little one   We had a couple of caravans; using one to house the apprentices, and the other to have a kitchen/dining area. The weather favoured us but, as always, the builders did not!   At one stage they downed tools when only the rafters were in place, leaving the upstairs wooden floor open to the elements. To this day the floor creaks loudly!

Gábor delighted in building the house. It seems that there is a genetic necessity in all men to construct at least one house in their lifetimes. My husband had all the drive and ambition to fulfil this elemental masculine purpose. Every year since we arrived in Newtown Donore he had built sheds. There never seemed to be enough. Now the sheds were put on hold whilst the house was being constructed!   He sweated and swore and sought help from every direction. Everyone who came to the house had to witness his agony and pain as he poured over plans!

With affluence, building started again in Ireland, and it became well nigh impossible to get people to milk cows. There was only one solution. We joined the Master Farmers. This was an educational service for students and farmers. Having done a course in one of the Agricultural Colleges, a student could then become an apprentice. This enabled him to watch and learn about everything his Master Farmer did during a year. He had full access to all books, both financial and recording. He had full board at a very reasonable rate and all the comforts of a family life. Personally I disliked this invasion of our privacy; I felt that it was a big intrusion and sacrifice. At times we had to feed up to four ravenous young men three times a day! I did have help in making lunch but otherwise I had to involve my-self in cooking – a task I have never liked. But for the sake of keeping everything going, I did my duty. The house fulfilled its farming role in that when we entertained, we were at the far end of the house – the boys remained in their usual sitting area.

As the decade progressed, confidence in the EEC (as the Common Market came to be called) waned and our economy suffered. For me these were the toughest years, especially as the price of cattle kept dropping, because we were unable to sell our animals which meant overcrowding in the yard forcing us to take drastic measures. I stepped out of line and asked the opinion of a consultant. He wrote an excellent report and Gábor accepted my interference with grace. We acted on the expert advice and sold some animals for a poor price, thereby freeing up space in the yard.

It lightened all our burdens to have Daisy to greet every single day. Bertha Usquiano came to help look after her for seven months. I must say that it was wonderful to share with dear Bertha the care of the little one. Our friendship grew as we divided between us all the chores of daily living.

Jeanie Rowlands, introduced by
the Reeces

Rosa in summer gear

Gábor relaxing in good weather

Daisy with Augusta   Daisy with Gábor

Mother and Daughter

197

Building house

With Bertha outside caravan

Seven months

31

As Daisy grew, I worried that her ambience was too rural, and longed to introduce her to the gentler side of life. I bought a piano and found someone, Lou Milligan, a gifted neighbour to help me relearn what used to be a great joy in my teens. The hours passed, as I became absorbed in my old passion. I took the two last school examinations, getting 92% in the last one! I found that my fingers were not as agile as before, and avoided pieces with *Allegro*, or *Prestissimo*! Yet I was advised by my examiner to apply for a place with John O'Conor, who was the leading Irish soloist, who had a reputation for being a great teacher. Needless to say I was delighted and flattered. There followed two years of weekly lessons. This was a turning point in my life. Very faintly, music started to come back, until it was possible to begin to enjoy it all the time in my head. Unfortunately Gábor did not understand and began to feel pressured by the green monster. When my father came to stay, he was amused at the fact that anyone should be jealous of a piano. I gave up my lessons, but, without my weekly lessons, I did not endure. I have not played the piano seriously since.

Daisy started school: it was a local convent school, called Killashee. Originally a boys' boarding school, the nuns were strict and brought out, at first, the best in our girl. When she reached at twelve the final class, the nun in charge was noticeably cruel to the boys, and Daisy became quite rebellious. She had been cautioned by the nuns not to repeat school matters at home and did not do so until she was much older. In a way she has always stood up for her rights. She has a strong, loving personality that is wonderful for those she loves. All these traits were prominent at a very early age.

For me, in the '70s I was lucky enough to find and make two new friends who, to this date I count as amongst the best I've ever had. They were Hilary Wilson Wright and Mercedes Egan. They came to Kildare at roughly the same time. Hilary came from the west and Galway. People from the west have some of the qualities of Peruvians. They have the same cognisance of other peoples' needs, and have the gift of empathy. I have had other friends from the west of Ireland, and they all possess this other world view of life. In those two friends I found educated ears. Mercedes and I helped one another through the childhood years of our children; she had a boy, David. We literally reared the two children together. Like brother and sister, they fought and made up, and laid the basis for a friendship that would last all their lives.

Hilary, on the other hand, introduced us to more and more people. It was good to see our part of Kildare filling with people who had interest in things other than farming; some of them bought lovely derelict houses and restored them to perfection. A person that comes to mind is Paddy Falloon. He bought Millicent, a house that stands proud on the banks of the Liffey. An Honorary Architect he was the perfect man to purchase a beautiful Georgian house that had been burnt down by some Dublin Jackeens, brought to the countryside for a corrective stay by the Vincent de Paul Society. Paddy bought the ruin and, with his wonderful knowledge of the restoration of damaged buildings, he made of it a living home once again

Friends from Europe sent their children to us to learn English. First came Ditta, a Hungarian girl who grew up in Switzerland. Her parents escaped from Hungary. In those days, under the Russian occupation, there was little or no communication in Hungary with the outside world. Those who tried to escape from this cruel regime were shot down if spotted by Russian soldiers. The borders were watched vigilantly. The small Vecsey family, the parents Micki and Alice, with their two daughters Jula and Ditta escaped in winter in the snow. Micki carried the baby Jula on his back. Hurrying as quickly as they could, Micki suddenly realised that he no longer had the baby. They had to turn back. It was dark, the snow was thick and they were in a forest! Fortunately it was not actually snowing, and, retracing their steps, they came upon the little mite, fast asleep! All ended well. They made a good life for themselves in Switzerland.

Ditta was a great success; we shared her with other people who had children of her age. It was through knowing her that we took on more youngsters, all Hungarians. They became our way of helping those who had suffered at the hands of the Russians. English had become a very important language for Central Europeans, as the emphasis on Russia as their cultural capital changed. Behind the Iron Curtain, no foreign language other than Russian was taught. If there were any tendency to go further afield, Chinese and Japanese seemed to be the only options. Russian soldiers on the street, armed police, massive guard dogs in suburban homes all pointed to the oppression being experienced by the people of Hungary. Naturally the children of our friends, constantly bombarded with an anti-western propaganda in the guise of education, needed to find out for themselves by going abroad and testing our Irish waters. They gave us great pleasure over the years. But I am creeping into the '90s!

Daisy 1979

A pony called Snowy

Happy girl

Augusta and Rosa

Daisy 1st Communion

Sportsday in Killashee

A wonderful day at the RDS

An aerial photograph of the farm and house

32

Our herd kept improving. We won at shows and filled a room in our house with rosettes. Silverware also accumulated, and with these came acclamation. We were proud of our achievements. Each year our holiday would be a trip to Birmingham and the Royal Show, staying with my sister and her husband, Ann and Antony Sabin. These were happy days. We met some of their friends, and enjoyed their lovely house in the Cotswolds. The cows we saw at the Royal Show were some of the best in the world, and we of the British Friesian Society were provoked by the Canadian Holsteins in the next ring. Little did we realise that they represented our future, as we looked at them as oddities. There was one man, a Mr. Ben Cooper, who was quietly importing them already, and was doing an excellent job. Gábor was strongly against their importation into Ireland! This was a battle that he would lose.

The Friesian Club was formed in Kildare in 1980. Gábor became its founding chairman, a post he occupied for some years. He subsequently served on the committee. He enjoyed working for the breed. He finally gave up when the majority of breeders turned to the Canadian Holstein. Although the Holsteins are far higher in milk production and very beautiful, he felt that the British Friesian was more suitable to the Irish climate, to say nothing about the calves. He strongly felt that whilst British Friesian calves turn into beef the Canadians produce nothing but bone and gristle. It is a long time since then, but today on a page of calves in the *Farmer's Journal,* the top prices for other breeds was over €300 whilst the Holstein Friesian only made €65. I would have to go to a mart to compare price realistically. Maybe he was right. I did not agree with him altogether, but, as always, he stubbornly stuck to his principals! This was one of the main reasons why he gave up milking cows in 1988. His health had a bearing on it too.

The apprentices changed every year. They were sweet to Daisy. The boys we had were all top-class lads, usually achievers in their studies, and likely to succeed in the future. I think that we had the pick of the bunch. Gábor enjoyed having them and teaching them. One boy told me in later years that Gábor had taught him to think globally. The same boy has since branched out, running farms on three continents. We feel proud of him, and others who have succeeded not only in cows but also in the horse trade and in commercial business. More have returned to their own farms and done well. Still more have joined the Department of Agriculture.

To help me look after the boys I had the most perfect person. This was Kathleen Egan, who had a great talent for making the lads feel at home, not hesitating to give them hell when they needed that! She was a Wexford woman, full of the skills that a convent-educated person had in those days. She loved to cook and keep house. We got on well, which was essential to a job such as hers, closely working together. I was very sad when she left, but she had given us several years. Nancy was with us again too at this time, and her little boy used to come with her on a Saturday.

33

In 1975 Gábor and I went to Kenya. Éva and Richard Pestalozzi were living there and had invited us for three weeks. It was a very special holiday. Richard was Ambassador for his country – Switzerland. They had the most beautiful house, with a guest house set deep in the garden. They had made plans for us and were delighted when Dad decided that he was going to accompany us. All three of us flew together to Africa. We left Daisy with kind neighbours, Haddi and Gareth Yates.

From the moment we arrived this was to be an extraordinary event. Our suitcases were slashed in the airport in Nairobi, but fortunately our clothes were not interesting to the would-be thieves. Nothing was stolen, and we were reimbursed for our cases! Such was our introduction to Kenya.

Leaving the airport was like returning to our beloved Peru. The same dry climate and dust greeted us, followed by the leafy suburbs that housed the Embassy. Bird song and the indefinable sweet smell of a hot country made us excited, and annoyed our hosts. They grew tired of our constant reference back to our past, when they were showing us their present. It is annoying when comparisons defeat reactions. We tried not to show our reminiscences, but, escaping to our quarters at night, with Dad as audience, it all poured out. What Éva and Richard did not understand was that we were at home, back to our years of honeymoon, escaping from our life of commitment to the bovine industry.

We settled into enjoyment.

The first part of our stay included a visit to the Mothaiga club, where we swam and had lunch. This is a typical colonial club, run by the British, that proclaims its ascendancy.   The latter always tends to bring out the Irish in me,–disliking the strongly white presence of the guests. However, Dad luxuriated in it, glad of all its luxury.   I kept my thoughts to myself, thinking that our Hungarian hostess would not understand.   Years later, I would know that Éva would have empathised with my feelings. Later we went into the city and bought trinkets. I bought a doll for Daisy, a little black doll.   Every day I sent a postcard to our little one.   Then it was time to go on safari!

Those wild animals were incredible.   Nothing prepared me for their dominance of the country.   They were not instantly visible; they had to be spotted.   Once again a representative picture fills my mind.   It is a giraffe in the distance, sparse tall grass in the foreground, tall thin trees behind, the giraffes grazing their topmost leaves.   I wondered for how many centuries this had gone on!   They looked gentle creatures, but I was assured that they could kill with a kick.

We saw everything; lions, tigers, cheetahs, flamingos, hippos and every sort of deer one could imagine.   My thirst for more could not be sated.   Gábor grew tired of it.   He would have preferred to have had his rifle!   We camped for a night near a lake full of hippopotami and flamingos.   Sounds during the night were eerie.

Samburu Park was our next destination and we stayed in the hotel.   Signs in our bedroom warned about intruding, thieving monkeys!   We sat on a verandah with drinks and looked at a spot where tigers were known to come.   The spot was on the other side of a small river.   The bank rose upwards, covered in bamboo and palms, making a thoroughly romantic setting. The tiger did not come that evening!

Next day we went to Mombassa, the coastal town.   Here we met a friend of Éva's a Frenchman whom she called "Henri cheri". He was a famous orchid breeder.   There must have been an acre of his little plants, each in its own special environment. Éva was delighted. She was a collector also. We separated for lunch. Gábor and I took Dad to a native restaurant. Sitting next to an Indian, poor Dad found the experience very unsettling. He had never had to share a table before with a man who ate with his hand and was very dirty to boot! It was always a fantasy of Gábor's that when he travelled, he must live as the natives do. This could be uncomfortable for his companions. My fault lay in that I should have realised that poor Dad would not relish such discomfort! Some of my experiences with Gábor over the years should have warned me. I had become so used to my husband's little vagaries that it seemed natural that others might too.

I often wondered if Gábor was influenced by his childhood, or if our constant frugality on the farm affected him. At one stage when he had had a very good sale, he told me to go and treat myself to clothes. He did not realise that I hated buying clothes after twenty years of being together. In fact, he was probably the one who felt deprived of fancy gear!

The Pestalozzis had rented a house on the sea with palm thatched roof, and a separate little guest house for us; we could hear the waves. We walked on the beach and sipped gins and tonic in the evening. Gábor and I talked together about our lives. We had not had such a chance in a long time.

On our way back we stayed with Pamela Scott, who was a good friend of the Pestalozzis. She had a farm and had been there for a long time. It was an enchanting house, full of her life. The young Princess Elizabeth stayed with her before she went to Tree Tops, where she heard of the death of her father, the King. I seem to remember that Pamela was in fact related to the Queen. The farm was pretty elemental, but it worked. We ate from a chicken in the evening. That chicken had enough meat for all five of us, with some left over for the next day.

The Pestalozzi family

Gathering in Barcelona of the Doyle family

34

In 1977 we went to a ski resort in Austria with Daisy. This was where Gábor came up trumps with the little one. He knew how to ski but enjoyed being part of the ski school that was run by an exceedingly pretty girl! It was a complete cheat when he delighted in accepting his prize for being the best in the class!! Little Daisy was of course delighted to see her father winning a prize. I ended up on horseback having felt quite inadequate on the slopes. I had never ridden such horses before. There was no way that they would deviate from the given path, or the given gait. Like automatons, they cantered from one corner to another, trotted somewhere else, and then walked. They ignored totally any aid that one proffered!

We have lovely photos of our little girl with Gábor playing with a toy mill in a mountain stream. I think that it was then that Daisy first fell in love with the mountains, and, above all, with skiing. She went with Augusta and Michael on several occasions in later years. She became a very good skier, and in time became a chalet girl. Coming home into Dublin airport I remember Daisy aged five having asked all the way about why it was we were flying with Swissair, saw on the ground an Aer lingus plane to the delight of other passengers, said "Oh there you are, my darling little Aerlingulus, there you are, waiting for us!"

We went together again to Kandersteg where the Pestalozzis had a house. It was lovely, easier for me since it was walking - skiing. There we met Éva's and Richard's children and had a great time leisurely pacing our skis in the snow. We brought a little friend of Daisy's from Cork, one of Dom Daly's children. She was a good little skier and had pleasure in teaching our one.

35

The continuing presence of the lads in the house eventually broke me and I had to be hospitalised when my father died at the beginning of the year. Years of tension resulted in six weeks in St. Edmunsbury's in Lucan. As a result, at long last, Gábor was galvanised into building an apartment for the apprentices. This was a tremendous blessing. After some fifteen years we had the house to ourselves. The boys came in for a hearty lunch but nothing more. It was hard to believe that at long last we could start building up our lives together again! To have strangers living in one's house is extremely difficult for anybody, but for us it was very nearly the end of our marriage. Asked by a young girl some years ago when she was faced with the same situation, I surprised her with my answer, that if she cared about her marriage she should say no. She took my advice and was ever grateful.

Every one of the lads with only one exception over the years was delightful in every way, but two rather volatile people like us needed space to vent our personalities without an audience. Gábor's increasing race chauvinism was apparent only to me, - anyone else who noticed it found it to be exotic. Unfortunately his new joy in being able to return to his own country also embraced disenchantment with the Irish. He took every opportunity to emphasise this by observing the actions of my fellow Irish. I tried not to care but exploded on occasion, whilst in fact understanding exactly where it was all coming from. The women in the Kende family spoke to him regularly about his lack of commitment to his own country. One of them actually said to me once that she was shocked that he had become more Irish than Hungarian. I actually thought that it was funny, not realising how dangerous it would become. This may all seem somewhat petty but at the time it was hurtful.

36

It was in 1981 that all the Kölcsei Kendes got together in Budapest for the official handing over of the letters. Gábor and I had not been in Hungary since 1963 and we looked forward enormously to the event. Arriving at the airport – a very small place at the time – we met Zsigi and Madi, who had come from Canada. Daisy was with us. We reached the immigration kiosk with our passports and visas, and passed quickly through. Gábor was last. To our growing horror, he was detained by the customs, and escorted away. A full hour passed as we waited. We thought about how the communists were renowned for sudden arrests, and had long memories about those who had escaped in the 1940s. After what seemed a lifetime a man appeared and spoke to Zsigi. It transpired that he was our host, important in the Government, and had come to identify us all. Gábor's detention had been made to ensure that none of us would leave the immigration hall. The lack of good manners in not telling us about what was happening was for Madi and Zsigi quite normal in a communist - controlled country. Because nobody spoke English, I could not enquire and was cautioned by my in-laws not to do so. Finding out the reason was a relief but not calming! Released, we set off for the city and our apartment.

Elsewhere I have described the events that followed, and the official ceremonies attending the handing over of the letters from Zsigmond Kende to Ferenc Kölcsey. The published letters were a wonderful surprise. We spent three weeks in Hungary between Cégény and Budapest. Lovely wooded areas near the road found us having our picnics, or we would visit small restaurants with excellent food. It was particularly good to be together, each with a different idea of how to spend our time. Several of Gábor's school friends came to see us, spending hours talking about their lives and his. The stories were sad, and full of death. Theirs had been a generation of terrible deeds. But they laughed too. Laughter and tears punctuated their difficulties. Hungarians are proud and not ashamed to show their emotions.

We returned to Ireland to find the apartment for the boys nearly ready. Eamon Dempsey, who was a neighbour and a builder, had been working away in our absence. The great day arrived when there were no more lads sleeping in the house. I remember John and Hilary Wilson Wright coming to help choose the plants for around the flat. They chose well – the same plants flower every year since. The planting was a celebration!

By now Daisy was nine, and still at school in Killashee. Pony Club and a good pony, Merry Legs, meant that she spent a lot of time riding. Her friend, Caoilphionn Rynne, and she spent hours together on their mounts. Events organised by the club kept them busy during the summer months.

The following year was when we seemed to win everything at the Spring Show. We hit the headlines in all the evening papers. If we had won a day later, the headline "Irish Baroness wins at Show" would have never appeared. It was the next day that the shocking news about Charlie Haughey, a Government Minister, broke. He had been involved in the smuggling of arms to the north. In those days the latter was REAL news.

We went to Hungary as often as we could during the 1980s - at least once a year. Gábor's cousin, Margo had remarried. Her husband is Éde Csorba, a lawyer, with two lovely daughters, Éva and Virgie, a son, and an adopted daughter. Margó and Ede have a charming house in the suburbs of Buda, near the Hill of Roses. In it they have a basement flat, and this is where we stayed on our trips to Budapest every year during the 1980s and well into the 1990s.

Many hours were spent sipping Slivovitz and Pálinka in the garden. Pálinka, especially from Szatmár is the most delicious 1st distillation brandy, flavoured with aniseed. They all spoke in Hungarian, and I amused myself by trying to understand. If we were there in autumn the garden was full of apricots constantly falling from the trees. Usually they had a party for us. To this would come all their old friends, and some of them Gábor's as well. Well known names, redolent of history and the past, it was interesting to hear how they had survived. I remember an enchanting couple called Pallavicini dressed as they had been in the 1920s, boater hats and pale summer suits. They kept themselves going by growing vegetables on a tiny patch of ground, less than half an acre. They seemed so very frail for such an enterprise. Like so many others they had lost thousands of acres to the invading Russians.

An old friend of Gábor's was Coci Genko. She spoke perfect English, a great blessing for me. Her offer of a bed was very gratefully received. I never had to avail of it but she invited us to dine every time we were there. Her husband, Tibor, was once a famous jockey, and, after the war used his riding skills to take tourists on horseback holidays. He was a typical jockey, complete with bandy legs.

There were many more, in latter years they included Lászlo Kárólyi whom we had known in Peru. After the Russians had gone he had managed to move back into his family home, albeit a small part of it. He was employed by the government as Curator. His wife is related to the Kendes through Margó Csorba. It is worth noting, at this stage that most of Gábor's close acquaintances, or friends, came from Transylvania. Transylvanians were known to have a world of their own! The Kendes lived nearby and were intermarried with many of this close knit community.

....

216

We usually drove our car to Budapest. It was an interesting journey to make. Driving across the north of France along La Route d'Anglais, we enjoyed visiting small towns, sometimes staying the night. These towns have been so well reconstructed since the war that one could be persuaded that the devastation suffered has been forgotten. Yet they do not fail to have their monuments, monuments remembering their fallen heroes. Those bullet holes in the walls of houses in Budapest, still seen in the 1990s do not encourage forgetfulness.

Driving on occasion through the Black Forest, we found ourselves quaffing wine from huge glasses. The forest is aptly named. Light is defeated as tree cover dominates. There we tackled the famous German motorways. These were terrifying, hugely overcrowded, fast, and by now, far too narrow. We gritted our teeth and kept a grim silence as we drove. French roads are far superior. I wonder what Hitler would say? He was so proud of his roads. Arriving in Austria we were nearly there. From here we had to gauge whether we should carry on to Budapest directly, or spend another night on the road. This depended on the hour. I loved it when we stayed in a monastery in Gyor, near the border, in Hungary. Beautifully converted for guests, it was so peaceful. Some of the old monks were still there. In many ways the feel of that hotel was for me the most comfortable public place in Hungary. Maybe it was centuries of godliness allied with religion that obviated the effect made by occupying forces. I never found out if invading armies had occupied it, but certainly there were no signs of them, neither in the cloisters, nor in the cells where we slept. It would have been a seen obligation for the monks to repair any damage immediately.

Miki Szemere, Gábor's cousin became a really good friend to us. When we left our car at home he drove us everywhere that we wanted to go. Thanks to him we went back to Cégény again and again. Once we went by train. (We were surprised at how comfortable the train was.) Miki is an architect, and he took us to many of the places that he admired. I remember particularly the Roman ruins that we inspected. They had been a garrison, reminiscent of the great conflicts and friendships between the two countries. Walking and balancing on the foundations that remain and figuring out for what they had been used was a real joy. He took us also to museums and art galleries. In many ways, when Miki was with us we did not regret the lack of our own car. An amusing thing was that it was at this time we noticed that Miki did not drink at all – we had to be told that it was because of driving laws. Now that we have nearly the same rules ourselves in Ireland, it seems quite a normal thing to do, but then – we were astonished!

On a couple of occasions we went to Vienna by train from Budapest, and from there to visit Gábor's cousin, Marianne Coreth. At that time she was living in Saltzburg, occupying an apartment in the big house on Arenburg Str. Her son Alfie lived in another apartment, in the same house. Marianne and Gábor were the last of their generation in the Kende family. It was always very emotional when they met. It was about a year before she died that they met for the last time. She had a great gift, she was an artist, and could draw buildings and children beautifully – we have a couple of her drawings. She was one of five sisters, Gabriel, Daisy, Helen, Erzsi, and Marianne, cousins to the Kendes with whom they had always been very close. Her children are Alfie, Peter and Elizabeth. They in turn have several children between them. Micki Szemere is a cousin of theirs – he is Gabineni's grandson, son of Mariette. Erzsi went to Canada with her Polish husband – Count Wodzinski. They had two sons. Finally there was Helen and her sister Daisy, both of whom married Gábor Szentpály. Daisy had two children, a boy and a girl. The girl was killed in an air crash in which she was an air hostess, and the boy, Gábor Szentpály, is a lawyer in Budapest. Their mother, Daisy, died when the children were very young. Her sister took over their care, and married their widowed father.

....

Margo and Ede Csorba were endlessly kind to us. Ede and Gábor never tired of talking, and forming opinions as to the state of the world. Ede told of his rather colourful past as he endeavoured to rear his children within the intrusive and offensive reign of Communism. It was difficult to raise them as Hungarians when at school they were constantly being indoctrinated with both hatred of the class they came from as well as everything to do with western culture. Double standards ruled the day as the children learnt to keep quiet about their father's and mother's points of view. Russian influence and occupation had been in Hungary for forty years, and it was difficult to try and get across to the ordinary Hungarian that people who had been landlords were not necessarily the tyrants and pleasure seeking ogres they were depicted to be by the Communists.

Nowadays it is amazing how Budapest has come to life. Gone are the days of the1960s when all one saw in those beautiful boulevards were trams, with perhaps one or two cars. Then was the time to see the city. Despite the bullet holes in all the walls, one could visit museums, and art galleries without parking worries. The old Palace had not been interfered with and remained in its original state; without overdressed waxworks; it left plenty of scope for the imagination. This is a personal opinion of mine. Renovation of ruins may be the right way to go, but, for me, the erosion caused over the centuries has a lesson to teach also. Perhaps this could be achieved by building a copy of what the ruin used to be, nearby.

The Hotel Gellért has never lost its splendour. Its indoor and outdoor pools, its massage parlours and its restaurants were all enjoyed by Communist bosses, just as it continues to be by tourists today and as it was by the nobility in bygone days. We stayed there in the 1960s but, having been warned about the peril of eavesdroppers and listening devices, I found it an impossible stress not to be able to discuss the days with my husband. We left, preferring to sleep on a couch in Margó's house. She was still married to her first husband then. Although we four had to share a room, we were far more comfortable with that hospitable pair than we could ever had been in that five star Hotel Gellért.

The Balaton, a lake an hour or so from Budapest, is a place to relax for the people of the city. Ede and Margo have a summer house there and we went, in the 1990s to celebrate Ede's 80th birthday. There must have been thirty or forty people there, and we celebrated with a goulash soup, followed by cake. Afterwards, by moonlight, we made a bonfire by the lake and sang sad Hungarian songs. Ede's voice is particularly beautiful. The setting was extraordinary. Walking a few steps to the lake we found it all bathed in light.

Next day we swam. Daisy and I had a ball, but poor Gábor got an ear infection that was quite difficult to cure. Later we were told that this is the one drawback of Lake Balaton. The water is too still.

A few years later we rented a house near Lake Velence. This introduced us to a completely different set of people. They were mostly tradespeople, electricians, builders and so forth. They became good friends, and we joined them in their carousels – they all had wine in their cellars within the mountain opposite our houses. The arguments about whose wine was best amused us! One man was missing, and they all spoke about his wine as though it were liquid gold! All the festivities were on the road between our house and the mountain. We did not have much difficulty in finding our way home!

37

Ever since we arrived in Ireland in 1962 our trips to Cork happened as often as possible. My parents were ever welcoming, and to go to their lovely house, Ardmanagh, was a joy. The luxury of staying there, especially in the 1960s, was a true holiday. Mum always cooked excellent food, and she was fun both to talk with and to go on excursions to shops, but it was with Dad that I went sailing.

Sailing had for me a continuum from my childhood that had never been broken. Once I was on board, with Dad at the helm, the sea around, I felt at peace with the world. Perhaps it was because it was the closest to *Being* within my experience. All life existed on that boat, and there was little point in worrying about anything else. This only happened on a calm day on a big boat. Years ago, it had been quite a different matter on my own little boat. That was all hustle and bustle! In the '70s I happened to be in Cork when Conor needed a crew. At the time I considered myself to be fit and offered to do the necessary. It was a blustery day on the ACE, and we won. I had to go home next day, but, to my horror, I found that I could not walk!. The muscles used on a boat are quite different from what is needed for milking cows!

Unfortunately I never had the chance to introduce Daisy to the joys of sailing. She did do a sailing course, did quite well in fact, but she never had the luxury of climbing out of bed and running down to swim and sail, only yards from the house. Later she would marry a sailor, and maybe discover what it was she missed!

We sent Daisy to a school in Dublin in 1985. With a background of death and mayhem on the streets of Belfast, and the discovery of the abuse of children by members of the Catholic

Church, we determined that we would choose a lay teaching school, and preferably one without too much political leanings. We chose a school called Rathdown, a very strict Protestant boarding/day school. It was a bad choice. Daisy soon found plenty of ways to rebel and was caught red-handed, smoking. I received a message from the headmistress warning me that if she did not stop, she would be expelled. I set off to Dublin. I have never heard such nonsense as that to which I was subjected that day. The poor woman found it impossible to get through to Daisy. She told me that Daisy was without emotion and could completely stare her down. I wondered to myself how she could be in charge of children, and suggested that the tenacity of Daisy's ancestors in holding on to their land for more that 1,000 years might be demonstrated in her attitude. Anyway, I went home, and started thinking about what to do with our girl. Suddenly I remembered Newtown School in Waterford. We had played hockey against them when I was in the Ursulines. We used to feel quite envious of them in their shorts, and of the fact that there were boys in the school. We, on the other hand, had to play in thick skirts that were cut below the knee.

Gábor and I had long conversations about this, and, finally, travelled to Waterford to meet the Headmaster. He was a man of great sympathy and agreed to do his best for our daughter. Later he would tell us that at the beginning they found her difficult, but, with time she settled into what was a far more liberal background. In Newtown she made friends for life. It was a happy place,and the students were given great freedom. Daisy brought her friends home, and we were delighted to get to know them all.

I remember her glowing face as she left the train in Newbridge Station. She always ran towards us expectantly and happily. This made up for all the weeks of her absence. I remember making lentils and rice, her favourite food, for her first evening at home. A cake too was a must! The precious years of having children live on in one's memory.

In Kildare "coming out" parties started at a very early age. I think that Daisy was only fifteen or sixteen when they started. Naturally she enjoyed them immensely. She had never imagined such fun. We waited until she was twenty-one to give her a party.

In 1987 Gábor woke one morning to find that one of his toes had turned black. We knew that he would need assistance, and called the local doctor. He arranged for a specialist to see him immediately in Vincent's Hospital in Dublin. The weather was dreadful, with several inches of snow on the ground. We managed to get there, and were told that he had to be operated on immediately. We were warned by the doctor that he would not do this by-pass operation unless we both stopped smoking. I agreed, and Gábor told me afterwards that he made a vow never to touch a cigarette again. The by-pass operation took seven hours, and was a great success, except that he lost the toe. We never smoked again. For the next eighteen years, with the aid of heart medicine, Gábor had no major incidents.

At home the weather took its toll. The lorry from Dublin that collected the milk found it difficult to get through, and our bulk tank only held 450 gallons. It was with dread that we started milking on the second day, near the point where we had nowhere to put the milk. Fortunately, just as we were about to direct the milk into a drain, the lorry turned up. The first thing that I had to do was to ring Gábor in the hospital to tell him the good news. We had another problem when the snow melted. The equipment we had that was perfectly adequate in normal circumstances was unable to cope, because the bucket on the tractor was out of order. The yard turned into a lake of black water. I rang the Yates who were amongst our closest friends, and had offered help when they heard about Gábor. They arrived with salvation in the form of two huge tractors with an enormous bucket, and a trailer – another person I have to thank, also, was Mum who came to help all the way from Cork - she did all the cooking for me, and, on top of that bought

a new bucket for our tractor. Thank heavens for good neighbours and relations!

Our cows were doing well. They were good looking and very
productive. We won at the Royal Dublin Society Spring Show,
and had plenty of customers to buy our surplus. The slump
that we had experienced seemed to be over. Once again things
were improving. But the dreaded Holstein breed was beginning to intrude! Gábor was still vehemently against the breed,
feeling that they were not for this country. He also began to
have difficulties with his knees and feet. Going down the farm
necessitated using the land-rover. He began to think about
selling the cows.

We set a date in 1987 for our final sale, but had to reschedule
to 1988, the year after Gábor's by-pass operation. It was lucky
since he was still in hospital on the day that had been planned.
I devoted my time, apart from the work on the farm, to writing
up a catalogue for the sale the following year.

The sale was a huge success. We attained prices that had not
been dreamt of before. Every animal was shampooed and
groomed to perfection, strutted her way into the ring with
pride, and acknowledged the crowd's admiration with dignity.
It was the only time that we hired a professional to prepare
them. It all went well, culminating with lovely speeches in the
Sales Ring, and glasses of wine in the house. It was a fitting
end to twenty-six years of hard work.

We kept the followers (heifers born during the past two years)
and had two good sales during the next couple of years. This
did not involve milking, something we could not have done anyway since we had given up our milk contract. We had far too
many animals for sale, and would have had to have had a second sale the following day, if we had wanted to get rid of everything. Their presence here also gave us time to think about
what we would do next.

38

Now that the work load had decreased enormously, I decided that I would like to do something that I had not done in my youth. I went to university, The University of Maynooth. I registered in September 1989, and took up four subjects for my first year, a necessity in the college. They were Philosophy, Latin, History, and Anthropology. They were four interesting subjects, and I did well in all but Philosophy. This I repeated so that I could join the second year. Fortunately I passed on the retake, and decided to do Latin and Philosophy at Honours level for the following two years. Philosophy fascinated me, and Latin was easy. Philosophy was difficult, very difficult for an old brain! I was nearly sixty when I graduated.

Meeting so many young people on campus was stimulating, but my chores at home still had to be done, and Gábor was not all that happy to see me leaving him with everything to do! This was not true. My trips to Maynooth did not happen every day, and I never went for the whole day. Studying was my main difficulty. I had my own little study upstairs, but, as soon as I settled down, someone would come up with a problem. These were the difficulties, but the riches that I was exploring were infinite. The college had a most interesting programme for us. Aristotle, Plato, Cicero, Plotinus, Spinoza, Nietzsche, Heidegger, and many more, all provoked thought and reflection. I was overcome by all that I read. Sometimes I so wanted to know more that I would stop the car and read, on the side of the road!

As my final exams grew closer after three years, I began to suffer from panic. It seemed that my brain would never function. I was quite different from the child that I used to be at school. This was, more than likely, the result of my age. At school examinations never worried me; in fact I had an uncanny habit of dreaming, correctly, about the questions asked. Now I became more and more confused as the dreaded dates approached. It was totally stupid since it actually mattered to no one else but me! I was a complete wreck when I went into the examination hall. I scraped through, honours in Latin, and a pass at Honours level in Philosophy! I had an honours B.A.!! Gábor and Mercedes made a great day for me at my graduation. I was right at the bottom of the line – all my colleagues in front of me, but it was truly wonderful, and I am sure that there was nobody as delighted as I to be there. The three of us went to dinner in the Manor Inn afterwards.

Daisy was soon to leave school and go to Trinity College in Dublin. She had grown into being a very pretty girl and consequently had a very good time with lots of boys. She really showed very little interest in her studies, and none of us were surprised when she failed her first year. Her subjects were French and Spanish so through friends we found a place for her to be for the following year in France. This was really good for her – the people with whom she stayed inspired her. It was a small hotel on the Camargue, owned by Denys Colomb de Daunant, a well-known film maker renowned for his "The White Horses of the Camargue". His wife, Monique helped Daisy with her French. We went to see her there and found the entire setting to be just as she had described it.

Denys not only did a film about the Camargue horses, he also had them for hire at the hotel. Daisy's joy was to help break in one of them. Years later, she was disappointed to find that "her" animal had lost its character and had become like the rest, an animal for hire. Her main occupation in Cacherel was looking after two small children. I was delighted and surprised that she did this job with enthusiasm and feeling.

Having retaken her exam, thankfully she passed, and did not fail any more courses during her university years. We never

226

regretted her time with the Colomb de Daunant – no university could have given her the confidence that a man like Denys gave her. She grew to love France, and returned to her studies a better person in every way.

It was Gábor's choice to buy Simmental cattle. I hated them – they were beef cattle, insensitive, heavy and stupid. If you wanted them to go somewhere they would force you to use a stick, something one would not have used with the Friesians. If they were standing in the wrong spot, and you wanted to pass, they would not move. Enough of that! The apprentices were gone, and only Jimmy Kiernan remained. Gábor chose him to look after the Simmental because he had a background at home of beef cattle. After spending much time buying in animals from all over the country, we settled down to breeding a herd. Little by little Gábor's health grew worse, his knees giving trouble all the time. This became really frustrating for him.

. . . .

We went to Hungary every year and enjoyed our friends. We went to a reunion of Gábor's school, in Sárospatak. This was a great occasion, and most of his old friends spoke English, which suited me. They came from every part of the globe, but there were also many still living in Hungary. They were an extremely interesting bunch. I remember one chap who spoke about the past. His father had been manager for a big landlord, and he told me how dreadful it had been for him to see his mother kiss the hand of the landlord. This type of humiliation had a lot to do with the eventual loss of the land. If the managerial and labouring classes had had sympathy for the owners, there might have been less apathy in face of the takeover; but no, one has to admit that it was in many cases the owners of land themselves who were instrumental in their own downfall. Their arrogance and lack of communication with those who worked for them proved fatal, leading to their own demise. In fact it was the reason why there was somewhat of a rift between my new friend and Gábor. In no way was Gábor guilty of what was inferred, but he would have been insensitive to the other man's sensitivity.

There were very few nobles at Sárospatak; in fact, in Gábor's year there were only two, Prince Rákócsei was the other. The fact that those two boys were sent there indicated parents who foresaw that English was the language to be learnt. Russia loomed, and the children had to prepare for emigration. Sárospatak was the Eton of Hungary – the boys even wore similar uniforms. They had English teachers, teachers who had themselves been to Eton.

39

There came a day, in 1994 when Madi told us that Zsigi had reached the end and was dying. We were really devastated, and immediately made plans for Gábor to travel to Canada. At this time it was still very expensive to travel by plane, and he had to fly through New York. It never occurred to us that he would need a visa just to be in the airport. All set to travel therefore, we were astounded to be stopped in our tracks in Dublin airport, and sent home, to get a visa. We did our best to get one that day, but, in fact, managed to get it the following day. He left. It was a good time to see Zsigi because he lived for another month, and was able to chat and laugh with his dear brother, Gábor.

I had left the college in 1992, and, once again, I was looking for something to do. First of all, I joined the St. Vincent de Paul Society, a charitable organisation that, amongst other good works, ran Meals on Wheels in the area. I volunteered, and worked with them for a couple of years. I took over the running of the local group of Meals on Wheels, and still do it today in 2009.

The Meals on Wheels did not take up much of my time, so, I did something I had been looking forward to - I took up the violin again. There was a violin teacher, a German, in a little music school run by Bernie Hayden. Bernie is a wonderful woman. She is a primary school teacher, with a gift for music. She decided that she would love to revive classical music in our county, so she started a school in a quaint little house on the Curragh. The Curragh is a large green area of commonage that also houses army headquarters, and is also known for the Curragh Races. The violin maestro was willing to take me on, and thus started me on a second try at the violin. It was fun, but I was limited by my age. I never reached the standard that I had achieved in my youth. I joined the Kildare Orchestra, and loved it. There were concerts, in churches and in halls, all valiantly supported. This carried on until, after a few years my teacher decided to retire from the school, to teach in Dublin. I used my teacher's retirement to retire from everything, both orchestra and lessons.

In 1996 I had a heart by-pass. Daisy rushed home from Italy to help, and Gábor was very worried. Having spent all day with me in the hospital, they were on their way home when they heard of a complication. Ashen-faced they turned back to the hospital to be told that I had to have a second operation. A few days later I was discharged from the clinic, and gratefully headed home. Suddenly there was a call from young Gábor, who was in Budapest, insisting that Gábor should join him there immediately. It had to do with the compensation that had been paid to the family several years before. It was a condition for Hungary's entry into the EEC that all former landlords should receive compensation from the Hungarian government. It was a paltry sum, sitting in Budapest, but now the government had devised a scheme that involved changing the money that we had received into a pension scheme. Gábor was in no state to go. He had been extremely worried about me, and remained very shocked. This was 1996. Neverthless he went post haste, in fact on the next available plane. In Budapest he was hurried from one office to another until he had done all he needed to. Unfortunately the young men, the other Gábor and Miki Szemere, with whom he was, hassled him too much, and he phoned me the night before his return to say that he was not well. I advised him not to attempt the journey, but he longed to be at home with Daisy and me. Kind air hostesses, seeing his state, looked after him. Daisy and I, at the airport, waited for him to emerge. Finally we asked permission to go into the arrival hall, and it was there that we found him, looking for his suitcase on the wall.

He was extremely sick, suffering from heart failure, totally deranged. A very kind airport official helped us with him to the car. He was exhausted, but longed for his own bed. We put him to bed and did not call the doctor until the next day. He made a good recovery but spent some time in hospital.

In 1997 we decided to retire from active farming and sold the cattle It was not a very good sale. There was no reason why it should have been since the herd was still a bought-in group. There had been a veterinarian strike in the Department of Agriculture that did not help matters. No animal could leave the farm until these vets had signed Movement Certificates. We had to keep all fifty animals on the place for about two weeks. A scheme that was the brain child of the EEC helped us money-wise. Called the Cessation Scheme, we would receive enough money to live on for the next seven years.

In the mid nineties Daisy met Nicolas Jacquier, who would become her life partner. I remember when he first came here with Katherine O'Halloran. Katherine managed to arrive a couple of hours late for lunch, much to Gábor's fury! There were three French chaps with her, and her daughter. A vision remains in my mind of Nicolas, oblivious of everyone else, following Daisy down the house to the kitchen where she was doing last minute preparations for lunch. They had been late, but now they were later!

After our retirement from farming we decided to rent a house in Spain, near Tarifa in 1998. It was to have been for two months, but more if we wished. I shall never forget that holiday; cold and windy, nothing to do. Gábor would not leave the house. We had our car, but he would only go to shops. In retrospect I think that what would be his final illness was affecting him; somehow although his brain was functioning normally, nothing amused him although it had been his idea to take a house in the far South of Spain. Illness or not, the best part of that holiday was arriving home.

Daisy was very anxious that we should meet Nicolas' parents. By now she had had a very romantic engagement on a beach in Corsica and longed to share her new family with us. They came down to Tarifa, by plane for a weekend. Dominic and Marie Christine Jacquier. Gábor managed well with his French – neither of the parents could speak English. They were good sports and did everything to make themselves understood. There followed weeks and months of preparation for the wedding. It happened on 8th July 2000. It was Gábor's lot to escort the bride to her waiting groom, a task that he admitted to me was daunting. Such was the difficulty now in keeping his balance. He managed it beautifully. Looking splendid in his new morning suit, he was a wonderful father and host to our 300 guests. It was on such occasions that he showed his background, kissing hands and bowing to all comers. He was full of politeness and kindliness. How the girls loved it all!

We had truly invited too many people to the wedding. It rained, and we had not really catered for that. People stayed crushed together at the entrance to the tent, leaving half of the area empty. The food was excellent and the champagne plentiful. Everyone seemed to enjoy themselves, but the crowd was overwhelming. Daisy got stuck on a stone wall and would not move!

The evening with 200 was a lot better. We had a rousing group of musicians, and a lovely setting. Dear Daisy and Nicolas were relaxed and happy. The French contingent dominated, and everyone enjoyed it. I kept going until my feet gave up. Then, exhausted, I sank into a deep sleep, waking up at 5 o'clock, when I started trying to get ready for the lunch the following day.

Some silly people told Daisy and Nicolas that they must not sleep at home on their wedding night, so, in full regalia, full of champagne, they walked to the O'Connells along the public road!.

No one had arrived to help at 10, so I rang the women who had helped the night before, to find that they had not realised that I was expecting them. Luckily, friends and relations rallied round, and, before long we were ready for the invited. Now there were only 100, and, thanks to Charlotte O'Connell who made a huge amount of kedgeree, we had enough to eat. Elizabeth's ham and salads were great too.

Next day Daisy and Nicolas left on their honeymoon, and had the most wonderful time sailing in Croatia.

The Jacquier family
Left to right – Daisy, Georges, Theo, Nicolas.
Tobias is held by Daisy. Liberty is on her father's knee.

40

Little by little, Daisy settled into a life of marriage in London. At first they rented a friend's flat, and then they bought a little house with two and a half bedrooms. This heralded the birth of their first child, George. We watched him grow, and saw that his character was gentle, and permanently inquisitive. An affectionate little person, he took all around him for granted and recently has been pronouncing judgement on his whereabouts. At three he flattered me by remarking, "I like Grandma's house". Such he is at the moment, and I long to see him grow and learn.

Her second little one is Theo of the beautiful smile. He is now four. He has not only a beautiful smile but also an incredible beauty of feature. Everyone enjoys him and his devastating looks. May they both have every happiness in life.

Little Liberty is with us now. She has just started school and is two and a half. She is a sweet and independent little girl. They were all here recently, giving me great joy.

Tobias was born in October 2009.

And so, life is again dominated by the welfare of the little people. Fortunately Gábor was able to meet the older children before he died. Photographs prove his love for them, his interest in their lives, and, above all, his knowledge that Daisy is happy in her marriage with Nicolas gave him great confidence in the future.

....

And thus I come to the saddest part of our tale. Almost twenty years after his first diagnosis of heart failure, Gábor succumbed again in 2003.   This time he could not recover, and little by little he faded away.   At first he was unable to stay at home and spent about a month in hospital.   Then, for three long years he suffered this horrible prelude to death.   His stay at home was punctuated by visits to Tallaght hospital in Dublin. Helen Erasmus came to help me in the house and to look after him with me.   Her presence meant that I could shop without feeling guilty and sometimes spend a night elsewhere.   His niece, Isabel, Bertha and of course, Daisy were constant visitors from abroad, whilst Hilary, Daniel and Graham were all to be relied on at home.   Clemens Matuschka and the Egans, Charlie Angel, Mervyn Eager, Joan Lambert, Audrey Johnson and Eamon Dempsey all came to see him as he lay.   Augusta, too, was constant in her attention.   There were many more, all showing their love for him who had taken life in hand, and was now bowing out with typical bravery and hope.   He left me well provided for and with memories of a marriage of great happiness and fulfilment.

I loved my Gábor as did he me.   We had a good partnership during all our marriage and managed to keep our love going too, despite difficulties faced by nearly every couple.   I could write so much more of him who was my husband, but I will say no more for now.   He died on 3rd February, 2006.   May he rest in peace.

APPENDIX 1

The following is a speech made by Gábor in 1984. The Kildare Friesian Club had him as its first President in 1979. Bill Twomey made his donation (from the Milk Board) consequent on Gábor's election!

Mr. Chairman, Ladies and Gentlemen,

Your Committee had the bravery to ask me some weeks ago to say a few words tonight on how and why I got into dairy farming and into building up our Robertstown Friesian Herd.

Now, you know, I'm sure, that life is full of events, some of which are planned, and many others that happen by accident, rather than by design. We also have to admit that our present does take root in the past, and that our future depends very much on our present. Mind you, - I really feel that this time our future is more in the hands of the E.E.C than in our own. In any case let me start by telling you where I come from.

I was born 60 years ago in Hungary, where my family had been farming, soldiering and politicing for many centuries. We owned a few thousand acres of land in Eastern Hungary – (this would be comparable to a few hundred acres in the Ireland of today) where my father, grandfather , and all my ancestors lived and tilled the land, bred cattle horses and sheep ever since they arrived with the first tribes to settle there over 1000 years ago. Therefore it is obvious and natural that farming and the love of livestock should be in my blood and form part of my life.

In 1945 the Russian forces invaded my country, and within a few weeks we had lost everything we owned – land, livestock, house, and all personal belongings, bar a few bits and pieces of sentimental value that we were able to save. A Russian soldier stood on the steps of our house urging people to help themselves. The padre's wife cleverly asked if she also could avail of the chance. She took two pictures for us, one of which to this day hangs in our house. It took many years to recover them, and the Hungarian government made us pay for them!

After some years the people of the village were ordered to return the furniture. This made them very angry. They returned what they had but dumped it in the mud in front of the house.

I was studying economics at the time at the University in Budapest, and it became clear very soon to me that I had to think in terms of starting a new life, somewhere else, where personal freedom, and a democratic way of life would allow me to turn my hand to anything that gave a hope for the future.

Just about a year after the Soviet invasion I managed to escape, and, to cut a long story short, I arrived in Ireland in August1947 with the vast sum of £14.11 shillings in my pocket and a suitcase of clothes. I was a refugee who found a home in a new country that was very much like his own.

There is a great deal of similarity between Irish and Hungarian people, - in their way of life and likings. I was to spend the next five years in Ireland, earning my living in many different and strange ways, especially during the first year. I was grooming horses for a while for £3.10 shillings a week. I worked on the docks for £14.17.8 (including 2d.an hour "danger money") – helped a builder in Co. Wicklow for a time, and mixed some terrible looking brew in big barrels with a soft drink company, who just about poisoned every child with their homemade squashes.

Eventually I got a job in Goffs, the bloodstock auctioneers, where I was to spend the next four years, in their Pedigree Department, compiling and researching the background of the entries for the various yearling and other sales. By the time I left Goffs in 1952 I had a fair grip of the "vocabulary" of the pedigree breeder, and an instinctive liking for the assessment of an animal's breeding value, through its pedigree.

Now, I am not saying that being conversant with pedigrees is, by itself, the guarantee of better breeding. One should, as time goes on, get an image in one's mind's eye of the conformation of as many bulls, - and especially cows, whose breeding one is familiar with. The greatest help in this respect is to visit the Shows, good herds, A.I. stations, etc.. Much can be learnt by paging through past Friesian Journals and other books, noting the breeders, relationship and conformation of the cattle from years ago.

I have the greatest admiration for people, like Mr. Seamus Kelly – whom you probably all know, - who has a photographic memory – insofar as he is able to remember all the better animals he ever saw, and instantly matches pedigree to conformation in his mind. But then, he is a man with a very special gift, whose success as a breeder has been proven over many years.

But there are younger people too who have this intense interest in Friesians. I once met a 12 year old lad from Co. Kerry, whose family are well known breeders in that part of the country. This boy knew not only the pedigree of every one of their 80 cows, but he also knew their tag numbers by heart. So you see, you don't have to be 60 years old, or more, to be able to know your cattle.

But let's get back on track. Opportunities to change the course of our lives present themselves to all of us. The greatest chance that came my way was an offer of a job in Peru, in South America. Since childhood I had been fascinated by that continent. This happened in 1952, while I was still with Goffs, earning the princely sum of £5 per week. The time was right for me to get off my backside and go out into the wider spaces of a far away continent that I knew little about. The job in prospect fitted my imagination and temperament and the idea of earning three times as much as I earned in my office job in Dublin, was too good to refuse.

Soon I was to start work as a "time-keeper", the lowest rung on the management ladder of a 28,000 acre estate in a remote valley of the Peruvian coast.

The estate stretched from the Andean foothills, some 30 miles down to the Pacific Ocean, where we owned our own port. The main enterprise was the growing and processing of sugar cane into raw sugar, but we had a sizeable acreage of cotton, maize, rice and other crops as well. We even grew avocado pears, lemons, grapefruit and oranges, coffee, cocoa and bananas. A 30 acre vineyard was the source of our merrymaking, because all the grapes were distilled into home made brandy, 1,500 gallons of it in a good year.

A 1,000 head beef herd and a 100 cow Friesian dairy herd provided meat and milk for a workforce of over 2,000 people and their families, a total population of over 8,000. The sugar factory worked 24 hours a day for 11 months in the year, foundry, workshops and garages catered for every need of the estate, and its large number of vehicles, tractors, rolling stock and other equipment. Schools, hospitals and welfare services catered for the population. We bred all our saddle horses and mules, of which we had 120 in use every day.

Once again I was back on the land, I was in my element in this vast place, which was virtually isolated from the outside world by miles and miles of arid desert stretching at either side of our fertile valley. The climate is like eternal spring and the people are friendly and cheerful. There were a dozen or so Europeans on the staff, most of them from England and Scotland and Holland, filling the senior positions of engineering, chemistry and accountancy.

The manager was a young Irishman from Tipperary, who ran the place like clockwork, and also had a great liking for good saddle horses, fighting cocks, and merrymaking. We would, on many occasions dance and drink in the village all night and go straight to work when dawn broke, because that was the time when work started in the fields, and, for those of us who worked on the agricultural side of the business. The hours were long, and the job of getting around *on horseback to see 600 or more workmen in 20 or 30 groups doing different jobs all over the valley could take 6 – 8 hours in the saddle. You had to take their names, note the nature of work they were doing, and, when you got home and had a quick bite, make up the books for the day, and balance the wages; all of it in Spanish.*

This was all part and parcel of my basic training to become manager one day. It took three years to be guided through every facet and all the activities of the estate, and, although it was a lot of hard work and very long hours, I loved every minute of it and even today I look back on these years as the best school I ever went to.

In this part of Peru, where rain only comes every 25 or 30 years, and all farming is based on artificial irrigation, it is of particular pleasure to see cattle grazing lush pastures. It is only during the summer, from January to May that the rainy season in the high Andes sends a big swell of water into the coastal valley to the west, and you can afford to flood your pasturelands and scrub to give a vigorous growth for a brief period. At other times the cattle have to do with being second class citizens, especially where commercially valuable crops, such as sugar cane and cotton are grown. But when water is plentiful, the rich alluvial soil is able to give up its nutrients all year round, and seven crops of alfalfa hay per year are the accepted standard and 100 – 130 tons of sugarcane per acre per year is nothing to write home about.

In 1956, having spent 3½ years in what was nearly complete isolation, I had my first home leave. I had become an Irish citizen before going to Peru, having spent the necessary five years in the country. My intention had always been to return to Ireland some day, and make Ireland my home. I spent a month of my three month's holiday visiting sugar plantations and cattle ranches in Brasil and the Carribbean Islands, and when I eventually landed in Shannon in the middle of June, the sight of the lush fields of grass, and shiny cattle filled me with an irresistible longing to own a share of it myself one day.

A week after I got back to Dublin, I met a pretty girl in the Shelbourne bar. After a quick lunch in Jammets we were off to the races at Phoenix Park. The races over, I asked her to marry me. Convincing her parents took a bit longer, but we got engaged in a fortnight and were married within a month, just in time for a quick honeymoon, and then to catch the boat from Liverpool back to Peru. I was to take on the management of the estate on my arrival.

My wife Rosa and I spent six more years in Peru together, sharing the joys and hardships that come from strain and responsibility. Whenever we had time we travelled far and wide in the mountains and the jungle, fascinated by the landscape and the people. We were in fact toying with the idea of buying some land there and carving a cattle ranch out of the jungle. You could buy no-man's-land from the government in those days for a dollar a hectare, up to 1000 hectares per person. But dreams don't come true unless you pursue them relentlessly. The years passed quickly, we spent another long holiday in Ireland in 1959.

We travelled all over the country and saw an agricultural activity that was just beginning to waken after a long sleep. Silage making was just starting and there was a great awareness of treating grass as a crop. I felt at home, because sugarcane is also a variety of grass, and I understood what makes it tick. I was determined now to come back to Ireland after one more stint in Peru. My wife would have preferred to stay in South America, she loved the climate and the people, and has a basic pioneering spirit. I had already satisfied most of my pioneering ambitions since I left Hungary, and was anxious to settle closer to my country amongst a people I could identify with!

Political events that followed in the early' 60s in South America were to give my side of the argument a push. Our company changed from British to American ownership in 1958 and big changes began to take place under an umbrella of mordernisation. Somehow this "Coca-Cola" civilisation always manages to wreck the spirit of a place. We stayed until 1962, and decided to return to Ireland and to buy a small farm that we could develop little by little.

I spent some months looking for a job but, at that time it was difficult to find anything. In the end I gave up and was just about to go abroad again, - this time to Mozambique to manage estates of the Sena Sugar Company, - a really plum job. A phone call came one night from a friend, who was anxious for us to stay here. He had just seen a farm for sale near Naas, and he knew that it had good potential. The next day we came to see the place, a thatched house without electricity, running water, or telephone, a four-span hayshed with a lean-to and three separate cow-byres with a bucket plant to milk 34 cows; Plus 134 acres of good land.

We did not hesitate, and bought the farm within a week, spending every penny we had made abroad. Then we borrowed some more to buy the livestock and equipment, - lock, stock, and barrel. The reasoning was that if our predecessor could rear 13 children on the place, surely we will manage to make a living. On 1st September, 1962 we moved in and the Robertstown Herd was started.

I needn't go into the details of the sort of life and conditions we struggled with in the initial stage. There is little pleasure in cranking a TVO engine of a milking machine at 5.30 am when it hates to start as much as you do, or to sit in a breezy cabin at the bottom of your garden, on a wet morning, because that is the only bathroom facility you have. But we managed to keep our spirits up.

Within a few months we replaced the cows we had bought with pedigree Friesians. The incoming animals all came from good herds, Cunniamstown, Tillystown, and Saintfield in the north. The Whitehead bull was the first to go, and was replaced by Moneymore Victory. I could go on and on about the breeding and upgrading of our cows and bulls, but enough to say that the essence of our selection was a good milking ability coupled with docile temperament in the initial years. Any nervous or bad-tempered cow went out like a flash. I hate them.

We recorded our herd, of course, from the first month onward, - even the Shorthorns. This enabled us to grade up any cow or heifer that wasn't in the Pedigree Book, and to build up a comprehensive record of every female in the herd, for every generation.   Next we started to concentrate our attention on Brucellosis, - we never had a problem, but we felt that if got into trouble, we would have to give up farming altogether due to big financial commitments.   So we tested privately, at our own expence, but it was better than losing everything.   In 1973 we became certified brucellosis free, probably due to the fact that we bred all our own replacements.

They say it takes 25 years to build a herd of good cattle – this would be about 10 generations – if we allow an average of 2.5 years for a heifer to come into milk.   I think it can be done in less time, possibly 6 or7 generations,- depending on what sort of stock you start with and how lucky you are with your selections of sires.   It is not a question of money – rather one of interest and dedication.

The first ten years were difficult ones for us, since we had very little capital to start with, and there was so much to be done on every front to enable us to increase productivity.   I would describe those years in the '60s as ones of hard labour coupled to a running battle with our various bank managers.   We were notorious shed-builders, although we couldn't afford it, but we knew that sooner or later, Ireland would be joining the Common Market, and we wanted to meet it in full production.

Our credit ran dry in 1968, and I took a job in north County Dublin, driving 90 miles a day, and Rosa ran the farm with the help of a local man.   We kept this pace up for three years, and we managed to put up a milking parlour, and to keep the bank in check.   We could milk more cows now, and look after them better.   But the pace was too hot – I ended up in hospital with ulcers, and had to give up the job and return to farming.   But things began to look up, - the early '70s were years of hope - we soon joined the EEC.

Now it was time to rebuild the house with more creature comforts.   It was a big change for us not having to listen to the sound of scrambling mice and rats in the attic when we retired to bed in the evening.

The' 70s were good years – the EEC gave us plenty of encouragement to invest in the future.

Looking back over the years, I feel that very great credit is due to our farm apprentices, who have all understood the basic need for better stockmanship. They have helped us in looking after our cattle, and we have helped them to be better farmers. Another person who had deeper understanding of the needs of a dairy cow than anyone I ever met, was our great friend and vet, Michael Roe.

Whilst I was putting down my thoughts, I was interrupted by a cow calving. She had a heifer calf, I am glad to say – the 904th heifer born into the Robertstown Herd out of a total of 1,792 calvings since 1st September, 1962. It looks like a smashing good calf, with good plates and nice teat placements. The mother is a RMX VG cow, approaching the 50 ton production mark. And, would you believe it, I had the audacity 9 months ago to mate her to a young, unproven bull of my own? But then, this is what breeding is all about.

Appendix 2

Appendix 2, written to our friends around the world in Christmas, 1989

Believe it or not, WE SOLD THE COWS! The reason was mainly an excellent offer to dairy farmers in general by the EEC – to compensate those milk producers who give up milk production on 1st April '88. We have been thinking for the past few years that some day we would like to take things a bit easier,- this was the perfect opportunity to get rid of the drudgery and even get paid for doing so. We held the dispersal sale of our milking herd – some 75 head – at the end of March and had a huge crowd of buyers outbidding one another to b ring home our cows. It was a great consolation to know that nearly all the animals were bought by some of the best pedigree breeders in the country.

Now we are at the very beginning of building up a beef herd, - it will take several years for the changeover, as we still have a number of Friesian heifers to bring to saleable age. Nevertheless the work load has diminished considerably, and we have only one man working with us now.

In May Rosa and I spent 14 days on the Costa del Sol in Spain. Pat and Jean Vigors have been living there for a number of years and they very kindly arranged for us to stay in a splendid apartment on the beach at Sotogrande. Although the weather was not warm enough for bathing, we had a rented car and enjoyed enormously driving around in the Sierra just north of the costa. – the wild flowers are in full blaze that time of year, and the scenery is simply magnificent.

The summer was spent with family visitors who came to share our newly found freedom, and the occasional short trip to some part of Ireland that we had not been to before. We have become quite mobile – within the confines of Ireland of course, and often visit Daisy on a Sunday in Waterford, taking her out to lunch. She has been at Newtown School – an old Quaker establishment – since September 1987. It is a mixed school and has a relatively free and easy atmosphere. Daisy has become quite a big girl in the last year, - mind you, she will be 17 next March. She is allowed home every 3rd weekend, when she takes the train with her best friend who is a neighbour's daughter. Last summer she went to two formal parties and has a few invitations during Christmas holidays as. We were quite happy with her Intermediate Exam results last June – she is a good all rounder. Her favourite sports are riding and skiing, - neither of them competitively. She will be going to Austria with her school before Easter next year. We might be going to Hungary in June

All that remains for us to do now is to wish you all a VERY HAPPY CHRISTMAS AND A PROSPEROUS NEW YEAR, and send you lots of love, Gábor and Rosa

Appendix 3

The following interview was undertaken by Katalina Palmai, wife to the Hungarian Ambassador. She took a Master's degree in UCD on the subject of how Hungarians adapted to being in Ireland for more than twenty years. The interview took place in the presence of Gábor, Rosa and Katy.

Gábor, a Hungarian Baron, his wife Rosa is an Irish woman.

The interview was conducted in Naas, Co. Kildare, 16th March, 2005. Gábor arrived in Ireland 12th August 1947. He married an Irish woman.

K: *How old were you when you arrived in Ireland?*
G: *I was in my twenties.*

K: *How would you rate your English when you first arrived in Ireland?*
G: *If you based it on 100% then I probably had 35%.*

K: *How did you learn English?*
G: *I went to school in Hungary, in Sarospatak*that had an English faculty at that time, and in 1942 I completed my Leaving Certificate there. I finished my third level education in the Jozsef Nador Polytechnic University, you know, in front of the Gelert.....my room number was 19.*

K: *Why did you leave Hungary?*
G: *When the communists took over our country in the 1940s, my father was forced to leave his house, and only one room was left for*

*   Sarospatak in Hungary had a Calvinist theological Academy from 1500AD

us. We left the country and moved to Budapest, where we took refuge in my aunt's house. It sounds exaggerated, but I really felt that if I couldn't be a free citizen in my own country and was about to be turned into a labourer, then I could not continue to live in Hungary. I should give myself a chance, and freedom was the dearest thing for me. One of my brothers was killed in the war,- he was very young, in fact he was the youngest Hungarian lieutenant at that time. So I had to leave Hungary. I just felt it.

K. **Where did you emigrate at first?**
G. I went to Vienna with my friend, we went to the border of freedom. It was 26th January, 1946. We went there ....to the other side of the river Danube........to the American occupied western Austria. I had relations there, so, with their help we later left Vienna...and then we got out on 29th February, 1947, in the evening at about 8 p.m.

K. **And why did you come to Ireland?**
G. In Hungary my family was related to a family (the Horthys). Within this family was my girlfriend at the time. Her grandfather was the Regent Horthy. She was my main focus at the time. She lived in Austria and had connections in Ireland.

What was Ireland like at the time?
Well, it was terribly backward. You wouldn't believe that it was an European country. On my way here to Ireland I had become somewhat used to a western type of architecture, and the general way of life, and, in comparison with these countries Ireland was completely different. I found Irish architecture very primitive. There were only a few nice buildings here.

And how did you find the Irish people?
G. Oh, they were very kind and helpful, and absolutely charming.

What did Irish people know about Hungary at that time?
Well it really depended on the education that the person had had. People in the lower financial classes hardly had the means to finish

their primary education. They knew nothing about Hungary. But we can't blame them. Those who were educated, and were members of an older generation, that were more tied up with the history of European culture, knew much about Hungary, and were able to recall their connections in the past. The person who was most admired in Ireland was Empress Elizabeth, the wife of the Austrian- Hungarian Emperor, Franz Joseph, who used to come with her friends from Austria to hunt foxes in Ireland. She always had wonderful horses of course. Irish people in the 1940s spoke of these memories of the past.

Did you see significant differences between the Irish and yourself when you arrived?
No, Irish people are so similar to Hungarians. It was not difficult to find a home in Ireland. But I realised that the Irish have a certain amount of hiding behind their smiles, which Hungarians don't have.

Did you feel confident about interacting with majority society?
G. You mean the Irish people in general? It was just perfect. I loved the people straight away, and they made a great connection to me.

K. Did you realise any distinction, prejudice in the course of you relationship with Irish prejudice in the course of your relationship with Irish people - because you came from Eastern Europe?
G. No, never

K. Did you have and do you have regular contact with the Hungarian community in Ireland?
G. We had only a few Hungarian friends who arrived in Ireland in the 1940s and 1950s

K How did it affect you when the Hungarian embassy opened in Ireland?
I always felt that I was Hungarian enough in myself. I didn't need other people to contribute to it. But we went to the receptions several times as long as I was healthy.

Do you feel that you have successfully adapted to the Irish culture?

Yes, I think so. I speak English, I read Irish newspapers, I regularly eat Irish food, but nothing else.

In your view, did religion play any role in your adaptation process?

I never adapted to Irish religiousness. I attended in Hungary the Catholic St. Imre College, and, later on, Saraspatak. I received a Protestant education. But here in Ireland I didn't practice religion.

Do you communicate with anyone in the Hungarian language in Ireland?

Yes, but not with my family. I never spoke Hungarian with my child either. She only knows a few words in Hungarian. I never gave any importance to her learning Hungarian. But I had a great Hungarian friend here, - he also escaped from Hungary in the 1940s. I used to talk in Hungarian to him. Later on he emigrated to the USA. Later I met Hungarians who came here in 1956.

K. And how could you preserve your excellent Hungarian if you didn't practice it regularly? Did you read Humgarian books?

No. But perhaps my Hungarian education helped me. In Sarospatak, at a very early age, I got used to being bilingual.

Did you have access to Hungarian literature from the beginning?

No, I didn't. I was not looking for it.

Do you listen to Hungarian radio, or see Hungarian TV programmes?

No, I don't.

Did you teach your Irish wife Hungarian cooking?

Oh yes, she regularly cooks Hungarian food, today she prepared chicken goulash for you. But she can do other things as well, like sauerkraut dishes, and many Hungarian cakes.

I have a Hungarian cook book. Last week Gábor told me that he would love to eat a caraway seed soup. He was delighted when I was able to do it.

K   **How would you describe your identity?**
My Hungarian identity was more or less finished in 1956, when I married an Irish woman. Actually I am completely international, and I am very much inclined to favour everything that is Irish. You can see my house, everything is Irish here. But I tell you something......If there are two boxers in a ring, and one of them is Irish and the other is English, I hope that the Irish chap is going to win, but, if one of them is Hungarian in the ring, and the other is Irish, I am anxious that the Hungarian will win. I still have a built-in urge.......A built –in feeling that you can never change.

He is 99p.c. Hungarian and 1 p.c. Irish. It is a question of breeding and a question of the heart.

How is your identity regarded by Irish society?
They never accepted me as an Irishman.

I think that Irish people who know him look up to him , and admire him.

K. **How did you bequeath your Hungarian identity to the next generation? Did you find it important?**
G. My Hungarian ancestry goes back a thousand years. I can trace it back to the settlement of the Magyars in Hungary. I preserved some old Hungarian books from the 1930s, they represent great value. We were offered a great sum of money for them by a museum, but we kept them. And my grandson carries my father's name. He is Georges.

What does your daughter know about Hungarian history, literature?
She is very interested in Hungarian history. She is living in London – she married a Frenchman and she is a member of the Hungarian

Cultural society there.   She is studying Hungarian at the moment.
I think she will pick it up very quickly.   She speaks many languages,
and she has the Hungarian gift for languages.   Anyway she is very
much a Hungarian, she even looks Hungarian.

K. Do you have in your home some memories from Hungary?
Not that much.   We have a famous painting from the early 20th c.
– you can see it on the wall.   Besides we have a few tablecloths and
Hungarian china as well.

How often do you visit Hungary?
The first time that I visited Hungary was15 years after leaving, in
1962, when my father died.   Afterwards we couldn't get a visa for a
while, but in the past decades we visited Hungary yearly.

How do you spend Christmas?
In the beginning we celebrated it the Hungarian way.   We had
Christmas Eve dinner.   But later on it was not convenient for our
friends, so gradually we abandoned it.

Have you been home sick?
Oh yes, many times.

K. You don't regret leaving Hungary?
G. No, I made the right decision.   As a matter of fact, I think, if I
didn't leave Hungary, I wouldn't have had such an interesting a life.
I have had a lovely life here in Ireland, and that was only possible
because I left Hungary for a free world, a world where I had many
choices.   In Hungary I would have had only one choice..

Appendix 4

Speech of Conor Doyle, Caragh Church, Sunday 5th February, 2006, the REMOVAL SERVICE FOR GÁBOR KENDE

I first met Gábor about a week before he and Rosa got married. That means that he has been part of our family for 50 years.

Rosa, of course, knew Gábor longer than I did. She had met him 2 weeks before! They were introduced at a race meeting and fell instantly in love. He proposed that evening. She accepted. Three weeks later they were married.

Although it is a long time ago I still have a very vivid memory of that first meeting. Tall, handsome of course. Warm voice, strong and relaxed. But even for a 10 year old boy there was an aura that hinted at much much more.

And so there was. At 32 he had experienced more of life than many would in 2 or 3 lifetimes.

Slightly faded Kende family photographs around the house of the 1920s and 30s suggest an idyllic youth growing up in Eastern Hungary on their estate where their family had lived for 1,000 years. While the shadow of war occasionally appeared I know that he grew up feeling secure in the knowledge that he would live the life of a central European grandee like his family had for so long.

The war of course swept away everything. The advancing Russian army forced him and his family to flee to Budapest where George, his brother was killed in the subsequent fighting.

After the fall of Budapest Gábor escaped to post war Germany.

While staying at a refugee camp in the mud and devastation that was Germany he had a thought or fantasy about Ireland as a place that had escaped the ravages of war. Green and unspoilt.

It's a long story, but suffice to say he achieved the impossible. He secured a visa with "pull". Put it in another way he instinctively and immediately "got it in one" how Ireland worked!

And so in 1947 he began his long love affair with Ireland.

In 1956 he came back on leave and, and, three weeks before he returned to Peru he went to the races. He set sail for Peru with his bride having a honeymoon trip on the Orient Express around Europe to introduce Rosa to his relations.

In 1962 Gábor and Rosa returned to Ireland for good and bought the farm at Newtown Donore. A sharper contrast with their previous life would be hard to imagine. An under-mechanised dairy farm where milking started at 6 a.m. to be ready for the lorry that collected the churns at 8 a.m. every day. No bulk tanks, no refrigeration.

They thrived on it. A wonderful business partnership developed between them. As soon as any surplus appeared it was immediately re-invested in new buildings or roads or fencing. The new grasses and crops planted were written up in the farming press. The all Friesian Herd regularly did well at the Dublin Spring Show. This was no ordinary dairy farm. It was their way of doing it.

After ten years things were well and truly up and running.

Then Daisy was born. What joy that brought. If one arrived off the road at 8 or 9 o'clock one got settled with a drink and immediately Gábor insisted that "the babie be brought down". He dismissed normal motherly protests with "but we were waiting for so long."

Gábor immediately rebuilt the house.

She was a wonderful addition to the busy house and farm. She thrived on it. Gábor of course relished fatherhood.

Daisy's marrying Nicolas and the subsequent arrival of Georges and Theo was joy beyond belief. I hope Georges remembers enough to share some memories of his grandfather with Theo.

It is said that when we get older we become, for better or worse, unashamedly our real selves. Old age is a sort of distillation.

Gábor managed his final years with great bravery and dignity. I used the word managed advisedly because he was always in control. His agile mind reviewed his declining body with wry amusement.

There was never a hint of bitterness. He was constantly appreciative of Rosa's care for him. He loved being at home and fully understood the demands his illness was making on his carers. The wonderful atmosphere of the house and the tonic he got from the frequent visits of Daisy, Nicolas, Georges, and, more recently, Theo, gave him great strength.

It all came to a gentle end on Friday morning when he died peacefully.

He has gone now, but he has left us with a lot. Friends and neighbours were constant and central.

The word neighbour was always spoken with special reverence. It referred to people whom one could depend on in need without question or vice versa. He loved the interdependence.

Whenever you call to that busy house, everything stopped for friends. You always felt at the centre of their world. This is an art he and Rosa understood to perfection.

He was a wise man with lots of common sense and practical ability. He was engineer, architect, builder, indeed visionary. Yet this did not extinguish his zany eccentricities which were so essentially Gábor.

He knew and understood Ireland profoundly. His forcefully expressed critisims never irritated because one always sensed his underlying love for where he lived

Yet his Hungarian roots mattered enormously. One suspected that he deployed his formidable will power to subsume his sadness at being so cut off from his roots. It was part of what made him so dynamic.

He got enormous pleasure from his Hungarian friends. Their frequent visits were always a special occasion.

When Hungary was opened up he was able to apply some balm to those old wounds by frequent visits that included the old family home.

First and last everything was for the family. His brothers Zsigi and George, his sister Éva, his nieces and nephews, Peter, Isabel and George, Balint and Gábor. His Rosa and his Daisy.

The windows are finished and the house is looking well. Gábor is gone, but the result of what we did together is around me. We sold Mullallys, the field across the road that brought our acreage to 150, for a large sum. Now I remain with 134 acres with tenants. Sometimes there are difficulties, but, generally, I am happy to have written these memoirs and glad to be in my own place.

He ignored personal loss and dedicated himself to research. He was my
husband's father, and always believed in hard work

It was in the early 1990's that Gábor went to Cégény with
Richard Pestalozzi. Richard was a lawyer and was the ideal person
to help in the final signing over of the house to the equivalent of our
County Council in the area of Szatmar.

This photograph, taken in front of the legendary tree in Cégény's park
includes local dignatories.